HOW TO AVOID STRESS
BEFORE IT KILLS YOU

How to Avoid Stress Before It Kills You

by Matthew J. Culligan
and Keith Sedlacek, M.D.

GRAMERCY PUBLISHING COMPANY
NEW YORK

Grateful acknowledgment is made for permission to reprint the following material: Portion of *Type A Behavior and Your Heart* by Meyer Friedman, M.D., and Ray H. Rosenman, M.D. By permission of Alfred A. Knopf, Inc., 1974. Copyright ©1974 by Alfred A. Knopf, Inc. Portion of paper "Regulating Our Mind Processes" by Elmer and Alyce Green, delivered at the Sixth Annual Meeting of the ARE Clinic, Phoenix, Ariz., January 1973. Portion of "Operant Conditioning" by M.M. Schuster in *Hospital Practice*, September 1974, H.P. Publishing Company. Portion of material by Neal E. Miller in *Comprehensive Textbook of Psychiatry*, Kaplan et al., eds. Copyright ©1974 by Williams & Wilkins Co. Portion of "Women and Men Said to Differ in Their Response to Stress" by Marianne Frankenhauser in *Psychiatric News*, June 18, 1975. Copyright ©1975 by *Psychiatric News*. Portion of material by Edward Greenwood in *American Medical News*, June 23, 1975, p. 19. Portion of "Stresses and Strains of Homeostasis" by W.B. Cannon in *American Journal of the Medical Sciences*, January 1935. Reprinted by permission of the *New England Journal of Medicine*, January 1935, p. 10. Charts I and III, Table I in *Preventive Psychiatry in the Armed Forces: with Some Implications for Civilian Use*, GAP Report No. 47, October 1960, pp. 265-309. By permission of Group for the Advancement of Psychiatry. Portion of "Biofeedback" by L. Birk in *Behavioral Medicine*, Grune & Stratton, Inc., 1973. By permission of Grune & Stratton, Inc., Copyright ©1973 by Grune & Stratton, Inc. Portion of "Comprehensive Psychiatry" in *Biofeedback and Medicine in the Treatment of Psychiatric Illness* by Bernard Gluck and Charles Stroebel. By permission of Grune & Stratton, Inc. Copyright ©1974 by Grune & Stratton, Inc. The Readjustment Scale Chart from "Psychosomatic Syndrome" by Thomas H. Holmes and Menonu Masuda in *Psychology Today*. Copyright ©1970 Ziff-Davis Publishing Company.

Library of Congress Cataloging in Publication Data
Culligan, Matthew J. 1918-
    How to avoid stress before it kills you,
Originally published by Grosset & Dunlap under
    title: How to kill stress before it kills you.
    Bibliography: p.187.
    Includes index.
    1. Stress (Psychology) 2. Biofeedback training.
I. Sedlacek, Keith, joint author. II. Title.
BF575.S75C84   1979   155.2′4   79-20010
ISBN 0-517-30556-9

n m l k j

It is easy enough to say that man is immortal simply because he will endure; that when the last ding-dong of doom has clanged and faded from the last worthless rock hanging tideless in the last red and dying evening that even then there will still be one more sound: that of his puny inexhaustible voice, still talking. I refuse to accept this. I believe that man will not merely endure; he will prevail. He is immortal, not because he alone among creatures has an inexhaustible voice but because he has a soul, a spirit capable of compassion and sacrifice and endurance. The poet's, the writer's, duty is to write about these things. It is his privilege to help man endure by lifting his heart, by reminding him of the courage and honor and hope and pride and compassion and pity and sacrifice which have been the glory of his past. The poet's voice need not merely be the record of man; it can be one of the props, the pillars to help him endure and prevail.

William Faulkner

Contents

Foreword

Stress is a relatively new concept in our culture and yet most of us will eventually die of disorders related to our inability to cope successfully with it. In an age when medical science has all but conquered infectious disease, we still find ourselves faced with the prospect of suffering—and possibly dying—from one or more of the stress-linked disorders.

However, there is hope; for effective anti-stress self-control procedures have been devised. Some, like certain meditation practices, have been popular in other cultures for centuries. Autogenic training, an autosuggestive technique, was developed in Germany some forty years ago, but only in the last few years has its literature become available in the English language. Edmund Jacobson's progressive relaxation has been taught in the United States since the 1920s, but perhaps the inherent simplicity of this muscle relaxation procedure has prevented its widespread acceptance in medical-psychological circles.

Now Western technology has evolved biofeedback—a technique for our time and culture—electronic, precise, and demonstrably effective.

With it certain stress-related disorders can be alleviated or even eliminated. As a preventive tool, biofeedback permits maladaptive stress patterns to be identified and then corrected.

Yes, we do have procedures that can enable us to cope successfully with stress. What remains is the difficult task of communicating this information. I feel that this book is an important step toward this goal.

Thomas H. Budzynski, Ph.D.
Director, Biofeedback Institute
of Denver

Preface

Throughout this book Joe Culligan and I examine motivation as a major life force. In view of this it seems wise for me to summarize my motivation and our intentions.

All doctors are severely limited by time, distance, and logistics in the number of patients they can help. If, through the medium of the written word, they can reach many times that number, the satisfactions are great.

Our intention is to present in a direct manner facts and opinions about stress that will be informative, motivational, and beneficial. Essentially this book has been written for two kinds of people—those who are now in a stressful situation and don't know how to cope with it and those who want to operate more efficiently and happily.

Using Joe's life and his interest in writing and communicating to others about stress, we hope to give you a real opportunity to evaluate the stress in your life and its effect upon you. We also plan to provide you with some practical and medical advice for dealing with stress or, as Joe puts it, for "killing stress before it kills you."

Traditionally there have been three major ways of treating stress: drugs, surgery, and psychotherapy (including psychoanalysis).

There is now a new treatment that we would like to share with you: biofeedback, which can work in conjunction with drugs, surgery, and psychotherapy and which may eventually replace all of these in treating certain types of diseases and personalities. We will present a great deal of clinical evidence supporting its effectiveness in the treatment of stress and disease.

We hope you will enjoy this book and that you will benefit from what is presented. A list of suggested readings is presented at the back of the book for those interested in further reading. We highly recommend *Type A Behavior and Your Heart* by cardiologists Meyer Friedman and Ray H. Rosenman; and *Stress and Distress* by Dr. Hans Selye.

Keith Sedlacek, M.D.

1.
How This Book Came About

Matthew J. Culligan

Some of you may remember my name from past newspaper headlines. For those of you who don't, I'll sketch in a little of my story that is connected with how I became involved in this book.

Back in the early sixties the Curtis Publishing Company, with such magazines as *The Saturday Evening Post, Holiday, Ladies Home Journal,* and *Jack and Jill* under its masthead, was looking for a miracle. The company had been in the red for a few years, and it looked as if, at best, several of the magazines would have to cease publication and thousands of workers would be laid off unless someone could turn the company around and put the profit and loss statement back in the black.

The board of directors of Curtis drew up a list of candidates for chairman of the board and showed it to advertisers, advertising agencies, editorial people, and business leaders. Because of my presumed ability in marketing and my reputation for salvaging lost causes, my name kept being mentioned as the one who could save Curtis.

In July 1962 I was designated president and chairman of the board. Within two years the company not only experienced its first moneymaking quarter in some time, but also began receiving large loans from the financial community as a result of my negotiations.

At the same time that things were beginning to

look up, a group, led by an unscrupulous man who wanted my job, was forming within the Curtis organization to get me ousted. When the internal warfare failed in its objective, the individual decided to carry the story to the press to see if he could damage my reputation and effectiveness (more about this story later). The media had a field day. For the next two weeks the struggle at Curtis was headline news.

I resigned a few months later, when it had become obvious that the barrage of bad publicity had reduced my effectiveness and the company's chance of survival. (The Curtis magazines lost over $11 million in advertising revenues in the fall of 1964 as a result of this controversy.) Even though I received a very handsome severance, I had a strong desire to get revenge. Also, I wanted to air my side of the story.

Unhappily, for many reasons, I could do neither. If I wrote a book (at the time Bennett Cerf offered me a $35,000 advance, but advised me as a friend not to accept), the reputation of Curtis would be hurt further, and its survival (and the jobs of countless people) would be in even greater jeopardy. Moreover, I stood to lose all the money Curtis had agreed to pay me over the next ten years. And if that wasn't enough, I realized that at age 47, I still had at least fifteen more years in the communications business, and potential employers do not take kindly to those who have spilled their guts without regard for the innocent parties involved and the businesses that would be damaged. I decided to grin and bear it—in other words, to keep my mouth shut. It proved to be a wise business decision, but I paid an unusually high price for it.

In 1967, three years after the Curtis affair, on my way to lunch at La Fonda Del Sol in New York City, I collapsed in the street, vomiting blood. I was rushed to Lenox Hill Hospital where I later learned I had a bleeding ulcer. It seems the acid from the ulcer had eaten into an artery, causing me to lose a third of my blood and putting me within thirty minutes of death.

During talks with my internist, Dr. Frode Jensen, I found out why I had developed an ulcer. Dr. Jensen probed so skillfully into all aspects of my life, including my work and my worries, that I thought at first that he might be involved in a research project, but I learned that Dr. Jensen had a natural inclination toward kindness—which drove him beyond his own physical capacities and resulted in a fatal heart attack some years later.

It was easy for me to open up about my past to this engaging doctor. I was the fourth child of five born to an upper middle class Irish Catholic family living in Washington Heights, a quiet and stable section of Manhattan in New York City. My mother's family, the Hogans, came from County Claire in Ireland and since the 1600s had been involved in Ireland's fight for freedom. My great-great-great-grandfather was the hero of a song titled "The Galloping Hogan," which I treated Dr. Jensen to in my hearty baritone.

I attended All Hallows, a Christian Brothers high school in the Bronx, where I was quite active in sports, making the football and track teams. One sweltering day I needed all of my swiftness of foot. Some clown had put Sloan's liniment in my jockstrap, causing me to run the fastest 100-yard dash in the history of high school athletics—back to the locker room.

Although I just scraped by in most subjects, I did excel in English and public speaking. My memories of those times, particularly the football games, are rich and good. A classmate of mine, Felix Tierney, had a connection with the heroic baseball New York Giants, which provided me with an experience I will never forget. I actually got to sit on the bench during a game and to visit in the locker room with Carl Hubbell, Shanty Hogan, Mel Ott, Freddie Linstrom, and other greats.

I graduated high school at the time when the seeds of World War II were germinating, and I decided to await draft developments before entering college. I got a temporary job at the New York World's Fair and had two spectacularly successful summers there in 1939 and 1940. My older brother advised me not to wait for the draft but to volunteer for the Volunteer Officer Candidate program in which, he thought, I might be able to pick a branch of the service other than the infantry. I took his advice, earned a commission at Fort Benning in Georgia, was assigned to the *infantry* in Fort Jackson, South Carolina, and nearly died of boredom.

One day an announcement appeared on the bulletin board, inviting physically qualified officers to volunteer for "hazardous duty." I did, was accepted for Ranger training, and had an exciting time and the most rugged physical experience of my life. The training was brutal: forced marches carrying forty pounds of equipment, survival exercises, mock battles, and a graduation exercise that left me limp and gasping.

I was assigned to the 106th Infantry, one of the new divisions, and one of my assignments was to give Ranger training.

Bored stiff again, I volunteered for overseas duty and was shipped to England aboard the H.M.S. *Britannic,* a beautiful and fast ship that, alas, could go only as fast as the slowest ship in the 72-ship convoy. It took sixteen days, ten of them tension-filled, to cross the Atlantic and arrive in Liverpool.

I guess I grew up on that trip. The unbearable tension was caused by the very active and horrendously effective German U-boats that were in the Atlantic. At least once a day the same drama occurred. There would be a general alarm, we'd all put on life jackets and rush to our assigned areas on or below decks (there obviously wasn't enough room above deck for all 15,000 of us on board). I agonized most when caught below deck because I felt like a cornered animal. I prayed a lot, exercised a great deal, and played chess, cribbage, bridge, and tablestakes, pot-limit poker, at which I made a lot of money. It was my favorite because I was so good at bluffing.

On deck, the scene was almost indescribable. The convoy stretched out beyond the horizon. Cruisers and destroyer escorts scurried about like shepherd dogs. When the alarm sounded, the escorts would careen madly about, launching depth charges. This happened several times a day. Less frequent, but equally terrifying, was the sudden appearance of a column of smoke, sometimes visible even before the sound of the explosion that indicated that a member of the convoy had been hit. If the convoy contained troops, the smoke column would be dirty gray. If it contained ammunition, it would be red and white. If oil, it would be black. We knew that soldiers and crewmen were dead and dying, and that those still alive, in the water, were beyond hope, because they couldn't be rescued. The convoy, in deadliest peril, had to drive on.

One episode left a lasting impression on me. During one of the alerts my group was standing on deck watching the scene off the port side. Suddenly I was thrown back from my position on the rail. I saw a soldier pulling himself over the rail head first. I hooked my arm over his legs, behind his knees, and stopped his rush over the side. He screamed, "Let me go! Let me go!" and tried to pull loose. The general shock wore off, and others grabbed parts of his clothing and we hauled him back. He looked venomously at us and screamed over and over, "Let me go!" We held him until the marine guards arrived, manacled him, and led him off to the sick bay. I never knew his name; he was my first exposure to a fear of life so great that death seemed preferable. This was my most sobering experience since the death of my father when I was 10 years old.

Dr. Jensen listened intently as I talked about my marriage, my children, and my business career up to and including Curtis. He seemed to keep coming back to the Curtis fiasco. He felt that my ulcer had been brought about by the combination of dieting, excessive intake of grapefruit juice, heavy smoking, a dreadful work schedule, and mostly, my continuing anguish over the Curtis episode. I was still suffering from unresolved resentment toward the people responsible for the takeover effort and the attempt to damage my reputation.

The doctor did have some hopeful news. He told me I should be elated by my innate recuperative powers. Despite the loss of one-third of my blood, I had needed no transfusions. He also gave me the indirectly comforting news that a healthy man who suffered an ulcer before the age of 50 would probably never have a heart attack if he reacted constructively to the shock and terror of a near fatal bleeding ulcer.

Jensen then zeroed in on the Curtis misadventure. Did I still "burn internally" when I was reminded of the experience? I had to admit I did. "Did the sight of any of my opponents upset me?" I had to respond affirmatively. One of these opponents was a particular irritant because we were members of the same country club, where I had approved him for membership!

Dr. Jensen told me I *had* to get the Curtis thing out of my blood, so to speak. When I told him of the offers I had had to write a book about it, he applauded the idea. He thought it might be therapeutic.

So I plunged into the difficult work of researching, writing, and editing my manuscript. The effect was almost magical. Without knowing the meaning of the exercise, I had overnight begun to convert the negative strain into positive energy. It was as if the acid that had caused my ulcer drained out of me through my fingers. I first used a typewriter with some satisfaction, but I found longhand writing even more therapeutic. At times, when writing about the more unpleasant details and the people I loathed, I slashed my writing strokes angrily onto the paper. One day, after writing about one of the more despicable of my opponents, I left my desk to go on an errand. As I walked past a mirror, I glanced at myself and saw a stranger. I didn't recognize my own face—at least it was not the face I'd been looking at for the past three years. The strain lines were gone, a half-smile had replaced the rueful scowl that had reflected my inner bitterness. I laughed briefly and muttered thanks to Dr. Jensen for his prescription that I write the book.

The improvement was continual, but there were times when I was not so relaxed-looking. A dear friend dropped in while I was writing about the leader of the attack against me. I opened the door savagely. My friend looked shocked. I asked why, and she described my white, drawn, angry face.

The treatment was complete with the publication in 1970 of my book, *The Curtis-Culligan Story.*

I walked happily by the bookstores, many of which had multiple-copy displays of my book in the window. The icing on the cake was the reviews. Only one book that season received more favorable notices.

The whole experience exceeded my expectations—first, in the reduction of stress, second, in the creation of positive energy, and, third, in my awakening to my potential as a writer.

It was enough in a short time to heal my ulcer and eliminate my bitterness. At the external level, I sometimes longed for the days of frontier justice, when I could have called out my foes for a horsewhipping. But even that desire abated as I came to realize and truly believe that in the long run most of us get what we deserve.

The mental and physical effects of the Curtis affair on me impressed me deeply with the terrible penalties of unmanaged stress. Since then I have become increasingly sensitive to how stress affects me and those I love. Because of an experience with a friend on the brink of suicide (related in a later chapter), I came into contact with biofeedback. I was so impressed by its therapeutic capacity that I co-founded one of the first biofeedback clinics in New York City. Our results in this center convinced me even more of the validity of this approach for certain disorders.

Through the clinic I met Dr. Keith Sedlacek, who was highly recommended to us when we were looking for a psychiatrist to screen patients. We discovered Dr. Sedlacek to be a remarkable young man with an unusual and varied background. As a high school and college student he participated in varsity athletics. In fact, during his senior year at Harvard, he was the leading basketball scorer in the Ivy League. Before entering The College of Physicians and Surgeons (Columbia Medical School), he spent two years at Harvard Divinity School on a Rockefeller fellowship. He wanted this time to sort out his thoughts on such issues as what can be done to improve the quality of our lives and the need for a holistic approach to patient treatment. During this period, he also worked as a ward attendant at a state mental hospital, where he gained enormous insight into the treatment and care of the mentally ill. He did his residency in psychiatry at St. Luke's Hospital in New York City. He is now specializing in biofeedback there and is doing a study on hypertensive patients. Besides maintaining a private practice, he is in the process of setting up a biofeedback clinic.

I hope you now have some idea of how I got involved in writing this book. Dr. Sedlacek is obviously the medical expert. He will relate exactly what happens to the body in stressful situations, what biofeedback is, how it works, and how it can help you. He will also give you some specific exercises you can do at home to help you deal with stress and prevent or alleviate the symptoms of stress-related disease.

I will relate to you some of my experiences with stressful events and the techniques I used to cope with them (some of these are especially helpful for business people). I will also identify some causes of stress in your life that you may not be aware of and give you some nonmedical suggestions for dealing with them, as well as offering you a more philosophical approach to life that might help you ease some of your tensions.

Finally, the two of us will tell you what the future holds for stress management, and we will discuss some of the methods that will help bring about the progress. It is our conviction that the information contained in the following chapters can do a considerable amount toward making your life happier, healthier, and less distressful.

2.
What Stress Is and How It Affects the Body

Keith Sedlacek, M.D.

The purpose of this book is to help you to understand what stress is and to equip you to handle it in a healthy fashion. All of life is composed of widely varying levels of stress. It is through stress that we develop and grow physically, mentally, and emotionally. Every activity we engage in and every force that acts on us compels our bodies to react in some way. For example, our body temperature is affected by the air that hits it, causing us to remove clothing in the summer and to add it in the winter. When we eat, our internal digestive process is activated to perform its natural functions. When we engage in sexual activity, various organs and muscles of our body are stimulated and aroused. Even in a deep sleep our brain is handling and reacting to the stimuli being fed to it. As you can see from these examples, stress is not only external and internal, it is also constant. During every minute of every day your body is under stress. This is not always apparent because for most of us stress has taken on the connotation of being something bad.

Stress is neither good nor bad. Elmer Greene, who has done considerable research in the area of holistic health, once said that the effect of stress is not determined by the stress itself, but by how we view and handle that stress. As human beings we either handle stress properly, or we let its negative effects get the better of us and it becomes *distress.* What we hope to do in the following pages is to show you how you can prevent stress from becoming distress.

Joe Culligan has shared with us a very stressful time in his life, when he developed an ulcer, which perforated his duodenum (upper intestine) and placed his life in jeopardy. He was faced with job problems, economic worries, his reputation being blackened, and unrelieved anger and frustration that were weighting him down day after day. Because of his vow to remain silent in the Curtis affair, he was unable to deal with the negative strain. Being in an essentially helpless position only increased his tension and stress, and his body responded by increasing its flow of hydrochloric acid, bringing about an ulcer—his stress became distress.

However, other than the stress-caused peptic ulcer and the loss of an eye in combat, Joe has had few other physical complaints. In fact, in his fifteenth year as an executive in high-pressure businesses (broadcasting and publishing) the sharp-eyed insurance examiners found him to be in excellent health, proven by the fact that he was insured for $5 million as a condition of a $38 million bank loan to his company. How had Joe managed to stay so healthy? The answer is that he has instinctively developed his own stress management techniques. He manages his time well, exercises daily, and obtains relaxation from his "catnaps."

Shortly after meeting Joe and hearing about his clinic, I decided to test his ability to relax on one of my machines. As you may know, the reliability of subjective reports of relaxation is very variable, but with the sophisticated measuring and feedback equipment now available, we can begin to quantify relaxation. I regularly record physiological data on my patients during their session, so I am able to note their degree of relaxation and their progress in therapy.

Figure 1 shows two electromyography (EMG) recordings of the frontalis (major forehead) muscles; we see (1) a patient's first five minutes of "relaxing," and (2) Joe's first five minutes of "relaxing."

Recording (1) shows the normal response of an individual sitting and trying to relax. The level of muscle tension is usually between 8 and 20 microvolts. (Two to 3 microvolts is usually a highly relaxed state. Readings are given in microvolts—a measure of electrical force—because the EMG picks

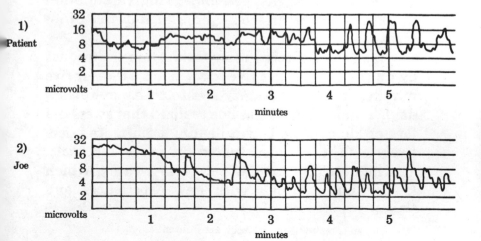

FIGURE 1.   EMG RECORDINGS OF PATIENT AND JOE RELAXING

up the electrical signal that releases the chemicals that cause the muscle fiber to contract. Thus the higher the reading, the more muscle fibers that are contracting.) Patients may eventually lower their muscle tension a bit more if they remain in this "relaxed" state. With biofeedback training, however, patients learn to lower the reading to stay at the 2-to-3-microvolt level. This patient's hand temperature at the time of the reading was 84.2 degrees,* indicating a mixed degree of relaxation. (Above 85 degrees usually means relaxed, and above 90 degrees means quite relaxed.)

In recording (2), Joe began to lower his muscle tension within the first minute. At two and three minutes he was already leveling off at the desired level of 2 to 3 microvolts. From three to five minutes, he maintained these levels. He did this without the benefit of feedback information and training. He has learned on his own to get to states of deep physical relaxation during his five-minute catnaps. This is supported by the fact that his hand temperature was a warm 93.8 degrees, indicating vasodilation (expansion of the arteries) and a high degree of relaxation.

Joe has discovered many relaxation techniques by himself. He relaxes five to six times a day for five minutes (a total of twenty-five to thirty minutes a day). Through his illness Joe realized that stress is a fact of life, and he began dealing even more effectively with it. He reevaluated his needs and goals, and he developed a new career in writing, which keeps him in touch with new experiences and

---

*All temperatures given in this book are Fahrenheit.

younger individuals. He also remains a businessman, but with a difference. He now looks for creative, helpful projects, not just projects for profit's sake. Joe has demonstrated that his motivation to reprogram his activities is of a high order. His appearance, vitality, and stamina are sufficient proof of his stress-resistant nature. The EMG tests simply confirmed my views that successful individuals often instinctively develop types of relaxation that work to decrease harmful effects of stress.

There are many specific life crises like Joe's that should serve as warnings to the individuals involved. But the situation doesn't have to get that serious if you come to recognize your ability or inability to handle stress and do something about it.

There are many jobs and situations that put certain individuals under greater stress than others are under. For example, Dr. Cobb of Brown University Medical School studied the medical histories of 4,325 male air traffic controllers. These men are responsible for successfully guiding planes in and out of an airport. (At Kennedy Airport a plane lands every two minutes while five to fifteen others hover above in holding patterns.) Dr. Cobb compared these men to 8,435 pilots who fly cargo planes. Although one might suspect that they would be under similar amounts of stress, Dr. Cobb found that the air traffic controllers developed hypertension four times more often than did the cargo pilots. He also found that they had two times the incidence of peptic ulcer and three times the incidence of diabetes mellitus. Clearly the job of air traffic controller appears to be much more stressful than that of cargo plane pilot.

The moral of the story, of course, is that if you can't handle a lot of stress or if you have a family history of one of these diseases, you should think carefully before exposing yourself to continually stressful jobs.

What you need to know and evaluate is *your* pattern of reaction to stress. Then you can choose wisely the level of stress you can best live with from day to day. We also suggest that you learn the techniques of stress management (many of which will be described in this book). By learning them, you will be able to lessen the physical and mental effects of stress.

To help you to better understand the effects of stress, we will introduce you here to two eminent doctors who first noted the physical and emotional responses of the body to stress.

The first is Dr. W. B. Cannon, a world-renowned physician-researcher at Harvard. During the 1920s and 1930s he discovered and developed the concept of the "emergency response." This is the physiological change that occurs in the body when people believe they are in physical or mortal danger. The pupils dilate, the blood pressure increases, and the production of the stress hormones increases. The body prepares, within seconds, to fight or flee. (This response has since become known as the "flight or fight" response, and we will refer to it by this name hereafter.) All nonessential activities (such as digestion) are slowed as the body readies its defenses for immediate action to preserve itself, loved ones, or an ideal (country, religion, valued principle, etc.).

When this flight or fight response is triggered,

there is increased activity of the *sympathetic nervous system* (the system that increases bodily functions when we are in an aroused or excited state) and decreased activity of the *parasympathetic system* (the system that maintains the functioning of the body in a relaxed or normal maintenance state). Thus the adrenal glands pour out adrenalin, and the production of other hormones is increased by the quickly reacting pituitary-adrenal-cortical system of the brain. This is a healthy, adaptive response to immediate danger.

Cannon's work demonstrates the close relationship between our reactions to stress and the output of hormones. However, it has become clear that if continually activated, this emergency response may cause a constantly higher-than-normal level of hormone production that will eventually cause physical wear and tear on the body. The person in this continually aroused state is then more likely to develop hypertension, headaches, ulcers, and heart disease and to be more vulnerable to other diseases such as diabetes and colitis.

Dr. Cannon's words to the Massachusetts Medical Society in 1928 still have great meaning for us:

> The doctor is properly concerned with the workings of the body and its disturbances, and he should have, therefore, a natural interest in the effects of emotional stress and the modes of relieving it. The field has not been well-cultivated. Much work still needs to be done in it. It offers to all kinds of medical practitioners many opportunities for useful studies. There is no more fascinating realm of medicine in which to conduct investigations. I heartily commend it to you.

Later in this book you will come across examples of high levels of stress and the rates of success that people have achieved through training to spontaneously interrupt their cycle of increasing stress.

The second giant in this field is Dr. Hans Selye who first noted and developed the concept of stress. Selye, in the process of searching for a new hormone, discovered that by injecting a rat with the extracts from ovaries, he produced a threefold reaction: (1) the enlargement of the adrenal gland; (2) a decrease in the size of the thymus and other bodily defense systems; and (3) deep bleeding ulcers of the stomach and duodenal linings.

Until that time these reactions had been believed to be caused by an infection or dysfunction of some hormone or organ of the body. Dr. Selye now suspected that they were caused by the exposure of the body to certain factors he came to call stress. He experimented further and discovered that other substances and situations, including an increase of adrenalin or insulin production, hemorrhaging, and exposure to cold, heat, x-rays, pain, trauma, or nervous stimuli, caused the same results.

He called this bodily reaction the "general adaptation syndrome." Selye came to believe that diseases of adaptation such as hypertension could be produced by abnormal or excessive reaction to stress. In other words, the body would increase its supply of hormones in order to be ready for action due to stress. Stress here means forces that bring about a bodily response that activates the pituitary-adrenal-cortical system to continue to produce ever greater amounts of hormones.

As a result of Dr. Selye's work, psychologists, physiologists, internists, cardiologists, psychiatrists, and others are devising tests and measurements of the effects of stress. We now have direct methods for measuring these minute amounts of hormones in the body. We also have indirect means of quantifying a patient's bodily reactions by measuring the amounts of certain substances (steroids and cholesterol derivatives) in the blood and urine. Thus studies on rats and humans can now demonstrate the actual effects of stress, its duration and probable results. In the near future we hope to be able to use these tests to detect the likelihood of future damage instead of having to wait for the onset of disease.

These diseases, such as tension and migraine headaches, hypertension, asthma, ulcers, sleeplessness, cardiac neuroses, and generalized anxiety, involve a complex relationship among the stresses, the emotional reaction to them, and the physical changes. Dr. Franz Alexander, a student of Freud and the author of *Psychosomatic Medicine,* was one of the first to discuss the emotional components of some of these diseases and their treatment. There has been great interest in this area, and in general these cases have been treated by psychotherapy, psychoanalysis, and sometimes behavior therapy.

The question that now arises is: Why are humans so prone to psychosomatic diseases? To find the answer, it seems we must look to our uniquely developed brain, which acts as the control center for the operation of our mental and physical functions.

Our nervous system consists of four main elements: the limbic system, the cortex, the cerebrum, and the spinal cord (plus the autonomic system). The limbic system, or the "old" brain (so-called because it is most similar in composition and function to the brain of other animals) runs the physical and emotional responses of our bodies: our reflexes, drives, appetites, orientation, and so on. The limbic system is also responsible for vital functions such as our breathing and heartbeat. Where humans and animals have the largest difference is in the functioning of the cortex, or "new" brain. During the time when we were separating from our fellow animals and becoming thinking beings capable of formulating language as well as developing complex societal arrangements, our cortex was enlarging and adapting to these increased functions. At this point in our development, the "new" brain (cortex) handles all our mental, or intellectual, functions—thinking, fantasizing, dreaming, talking, and associating—as well as our physical or sensory motor control: sight, hearing, smell, coordination (with help from the cerebrum). Although the limbic system and the cortex have different functions, they are also intimately connected. It is when the two get out of balance that we often have major problems. In many cases of stress, anxiety is triggered in the cortex and spreads to the limbic system, setting off the sympathetic flow. If this activation of the cortex and sympathetic system is continued, the body will wear down and eventually be hit by a psychosomatic disease.

But why do some people maintain or increase already high levels of stress instead of returning to normal levels? It appears that the cortex may be "trapped" into continuing a high sympathetic outflow, thus causing the limbic system to continue to its emergency response. A fearful stimulus continues to alert the cortex to maintain a higher level of arousal. Each time we see or think of this fearful stimulus, the cycle repeats. If the cortex cannot give up the picture, memory, or emotional involvement with a threat or even a symbol of the threat, the body cannot return to normal levels of arousal.

Thus it can be seen that the very gift—intellect—that sets us apart from the other animals also carries with it a liability. As our intellectual functioning increases (we as human beings can respond not only to the actual stimulus but, as noted above, to a symbol of the fearful stimulus), so also does the chance of our brain being shifted out of balance by the overcontrol of the cortex. Because of this it is crucial that we learn to regulate our reactions to distress and to not keep our body in a state of high arousal.

Another question that must be asked is, why do these psychosomatic diseases hit certain areas of the body? Often a person may have had a relative with a similar complaint or disease, so we suspect a genetic component and/or the process of identification (with that relative). Others have suggested that a region that had been injured previously may be "chosen" as a stress attack site. Thus Dr. Sam Silverman, a psychiatrist at the Harvard Medical School, "predicted" that President Nixon's disease site would be either the lung or the leg because of his history of injuries at these two regions.

A further example of the relationship between genetics and stress is the following case I learned about in medical school. The family of identical male twins had a history of ulcers. Sure enough, at age 29 Twin 1 developed an ulcer. Twin 2, with exactly the same genes, continued on happily for several more months until his wife, to whom he was deeply attached, told him she was pregnant. Later that night he was taken to the hospital hemorrhaging from a duodenal ulcer. A few days later his wife discovered she was not pregnant. Two weeks later, his ulcer had healed.

It seems clear that Twin 2 developed his ulcer over the fantasized loss of his wife's love, implying the fear of the loss of his mother figure or of the lessening of her "mothering." This "threat" acted as a stressor, increasing the sympathetic output. Because he was unable to turn off this flow, illness struck where he was genetically weakest, in the small intestine, resulting in an ulcer.

We can see in this case that (1) the normal stress hormones were present (as they are in all of us); (2) there was a family propensity toward this disease; (3) the proper activating stressor developed and was sufficient to create the ulcer; and (4) when the stressor was removed, the ulcer healed. What is the prognosis for Twin 2? An observant doctor should certainly refer him to a psychiatrist to discuss the causes of his symptoms. As an immediate measure he could also go for biofeedback treatment, where specific attention would be paid to teaching him to voluntarily lessen the sympathetic flow, thereby decreasing the acid flow to his intestine.

Often, however, there is no apparent reason for the choice of a particular organ or part of the body. In many cases it seems that the body designates some organ (e.g., bowel, lung, heart) as the target for pain and predisposed area for future injury rather than allowing the anxiety to be general. Fortunately our bodies possess a well-planned defense unit with many fine controls that, in people with healthy patterns, adjusts and heals the damage of stress. If a chronically unhealthy pattern develops, however, a part of the body may be in constant pain and the site remains raw and festering. When stress increases, this area becomes inflamed. "Cold sores" are a common example. The symptoms (or the physical condition of the site) may become so serious that a surgeon may cut the stress region out—as is often done in the case of regional enteritis (inflammation of the small intestine), ulcers, and Raynaud's disease—to relieve the symptoms and to eliminate the possibility of more serious complications.

Clearly your attitude toward life, your mood (optimistic or pessimistic), helps create the atmosphere that assists your defense system in repairing small wounds, bruises, and infections. This system also tries to destroy strange cells, such as those of cancer (including leukemia).

There is growing evidence from three sources —transcendental meditation, biofeedback, and the relaxation response—that many of these psychosomatic diseases may be relieved or cured by retraining the person to handle stress better.

We also are able now to provide physiological training for those who need assistance in developing their optimal pattern of old brain-new brain balance. Through biofeedback training we may be able to provide a healthy physiology that supplies the support we need to deal with the stresses and strains of modern life.

3.
How to Overcome Fear

Matthew J. Culligan

Josef Stalin believed that people are ruled by fear. Charles de Gaulle agreed when considering people en masse, but he held a strong conviction that certain individuals are ruled by other emotions—love, honor, patriotism—which at times overruled fear.

Franklin D. Roosevelt, in a statement inspiring for its time, but perhaps naive for the conditions of the seventies, said, "The only thing we have to fear is fear itself."

Unless there is a sharp reversal of form, it seems apparent that every man, woman, and child in this country will have increasing reason to fear nuclear incineration, premature death, injury, unnecessary illness, physical and mental disorder, loss of personal freedom and tranquility, and the destruction of material and abstract values.

In addition to the anarchist, crazed person, and organized criminal, a wide range of hazards and predators line the path of modern man and woman. There are, for example, drug addicts stealing and murdering to support their habits, and others who operate just inside the law, working their subtle, brilliant, and well-practiced strategies and tactics.

Fear, very much like stress, has two sides. The fear that makes one more alert, more cautious, and more defensive is essential. The fear that shocks us into inaction is perilous, even deadly. Fear can paralyze us by distorting our vision. Unfortunately, fear can invade the subconscious, so that even a brave person can be haunted during sleep or robbed of it by the subconscious alarms which prod him awake.

In Scandinavia they speak of the "hour of the wolf," between 4 and 5 a.m., when the nameless dreads, ghosts of the past, and fears of the future sneak up on the subconscious of the sleeper.

I have some credentials in the art of mastering conscious fear. As a child of 8, I fell through the ice in a reservoir near my home. I clung to the ragged edge of the hole, unable to help my friend, who panicked and sank beneath the icy water. Somehow, I did not panic and I lived.

On a transatlantic convoy during World War II, I prevented a deranged soldier from committing suicide by grabbing his legs as he tried to leap over the railing. Heavier than I, he nearly dragged me with him. We hung there for agonizing seconds. Looking down, it seemed miles into the boiling wake of H.M.S. *Britannic.* I avoided panic, and we both lived.

I knew all the fears of the infantry man: being alone, being shot at, being bombarded by planes and artillery, plus the special fear of being an officer with men under my care. Sudden fear, suddenly resolved, is difficult enough; the destructive fear is that which lasts for hours. I had twelve hours of that kind of fear in Belgium, during the night of the German attack in the Ardennes, the Battle of the Bulge. I was on leave in Liège, Belgium, having a hilarious time, when I was directed to a motor pool by an M.P. There, I was given a dozen jeeps, seventy-two soldiers from my division, and a map to the Belgian town of Aubel, the last-known base of my division, the First Infantry Division, the famed "Big Red One." We had just enough time in the motor pool to hear the nerve-racking news about the massive drop of German paratroopers in American uniforms. It sounded as though they were as thick as grass.

A total blackout was imposed, and we were told to move out. For twelve hours, traveling at less than ten miles per hour, we wormed our way in open jeeps, cold and miserable. I was wet, but not from rain. I was drenched by my own cold sweat. Just often enough to reinforce the terror, a sniper bullet would be heard whining by. At one point a jeep was sideswiped by a tank going rapidly rearward, and a soldier was pinned under the jeep and screaming in pain. His screams attracted the attention of a sniper, and a cascade of shots came at us. In every instance I flinched and ducked. I soon realized that this was stupid. Any bullet I *heard* was already past. I remember saying, ". . ., if I get it, I get it." That worked, and I made myself ignore the sounds of the shots and whizzing bullets for the rest of the trip. Incredibly, not a man was lost to sniper fire.

The next episode was the worst. A hand grenade exploded several yards from me while I crouched near the foxhole of my forward observer. The blast knocked me flat. My whole body ached unbearably. I blacked out. A short time later, when consciousness returned, I thought I was dead—I saw no light. But when I could move, I knew I was alive. I touched my face where it hurt the most, in the vicinity of my left eye. There was no eye, just a sticky, pulpy mess.

I felt my other eye. There was a bulge behind

the lid. The eye was still there, but I couldn't bring myself to open the lid. I guess I was afraid that if I tried to open it, the right eye would spill out like the left one. I got up and stumbled in the direction of our rear areas. The medic who picked the location of our aid station had done a superb job. Front-line aid stations, if well placed, were where a blind, wounded, or dazed man would wander or stumble by the nature of the terrain, like water running downhill.

I bumped into trees, tripped and fell, terrified by my blindness, but somehow I kept following the terrain.

Not far from the aid station I was spotted, and a medic rushed out and guided me in.

I must have looked dreadful, bleeding from innumerable small wounds, and with the ugly gash in the left side of my face. The medical aide gave me a shot of morphine. Its quick effect was miraculous. Not only did the pain drift away, but my fear, a small iceberg in my stomach, melted.

Hours later, when the pain returned, another medic prepared to give me another shot of morphine. Curiously, a whole new fear sensation hit me: I was afraid of morphine. I almost shouted that I didn't want it, but flat on my back, weak as a kitten, I got it anyway. Once again, within seconds, I slipped into a peaceful, euphoric state.

Late that same day I reached the base hospital in Liège, Belgium, after a long ambulance ride, with other wounded—many in far worse shape than I. I still couldn't see, not because of my previous fear that my right eye would spill out but because my whole head was bandaged.

The surgeon examined me on a wheeled stretcher in a long line of stretchers, much like a conveyor belt, waiting to be fed into the operating arena. There, teams of surgeons operated for twelve to fifteen hours a day.

The doctor examined my left eye and said, "Prepare for enucleation." "What the hell is that?" I asked. He replied, "What's left of your left eye has to come out." "How's the other one?" He examined it and told me it was intact, with no visible damage. When I told him I could only see light, not images, he said it could be shock. The nurse gave me a shot of sodium pentothal and asked me to count backwards from 100; I got to about 86 before going under.

The first hour after emerging from the drug was grim. I was gripped by the fear of blindness. Fortunately, the blindness in my right eye was shock and blast effect. When the bandages were removed, I could see. I made a quick mental note that all the terror had turned out to be unnecessary. Fear had run me for almost forty-eight hours. That was the beginning of a resolution I made to master fear, at least conscious fear. Within a day, this new determination was tested.

Because of my injury, I was due to be returned to the States as soon as possible. A few days after my operation, along with other seriously injured soldiers, I was scheduled to fly from Belgium to Prestwick, Scotland—the takeoff point for the United States.

Luckily I was classed as one of the "walking wounded" as we boarded the C-47, filled with those less fortunate—many missing legs and arms and some, I noted with particular horror, had lost both eyes—who had to be confined to a stretcher.

As we started down the runway and reached the point beyond which we could not abort takeoff, the field came under attack by at least two German fighter planes on a strafing mission (fortunately no bombs were dropped). I like to believe the German pilots avoided us; our plane was clearly marked and a perfect target. Because we were moving so slowly, we couldn't take evasive action until a sufficient height had been reached. Even then, fancy maneuvering in a lumbering C-47, loaded with wounded, would have been pitifully funny.

Up to that time I had never heard a sound quite like that of bullets whistling through the air when you're *in* the air. It was different from the whine I'd heard on the ground. The bullets crackled. I drove the fear out with feverish activity. I helped the nurses and the one male orderly calm the poor bastards who couldn't move. Their worst agony was immobility. They were strapped in and rolled narrowly as the plane veered and swooped. Some must have been in intense pain. The combination of sounds was disturbing and fascinating. The roar of the plane's engines, the crackling of the flying bullets, the cries, moans, and screams of the wounded, and the comforting words of the nurses were intermingled. I was deeply impressed by the calm professionalism of the nurses and made a mental note to marry one one day.

That experience taught me my second great lesson in the science of mastering conscious fear—the value of activity. Activity, the more consuming the better, is an antidote to fear. Scurrying around the nightmarish interior of that plane, trying to help others, was the best therapy I could have had. I seemed to be doing it instinctively, and it proved to be not only a help to others but a great help to me.

My life was virtually without fear for the next twenty years. There were concerns, of course —about money, romance, marriage, children, health, and the death of my mother, but little fear.

In 1964 a whole new range of experience caused a brief, temporary relapse into conscious fear. At one-thirty in the morning I was awakened by the telephone. The call was from a financial reporter of the *New York Times*.

Four days earlier, I had been attacked in a business controversy by one of my employees who was ruthless and manipulative. (As I mentioned earlier, I was at that time chairman of the board and president of Curtis Publishing Company.) In his quest to take over the company, this "gentleman" organized a cabal of other Curtis employees who were dependent on him for raises and promotions. Covertly he also tried to gain the support of one of the Curtis board members whom he knew to be unfriendly to me. When this failed, he decided to risk everything by enlisting the support of the news media to try to destroy, if not my reputation, at least my effectiveness in trying to keep Curtis afloat.

In advance he leaked the story of his attack on me exclusively to the *Times* reporter. This reporter, a basically decent man, saw in this situation a chance for stardom in the financial section of the *Times*.

The reporter's activities in this battle surprised me greatly at the time since he had previously nominated me as "one of the outstanding leaders of industry" in an annual feature of that newspaper, citing my management and creative achievements. Now he was to fall victim to one of the great weaknesses of the press—making headlines out of accusations.

The story was okayed by a member of the *Times* management, and putting the finishing touches on the story and sending it to the pressroom, the reporter called me. I don't know whether it was conscience or enterprise, but I know his tactics were unfair to me. He had spent hours talking to the opposition and writing his story. I can't imagine what he expected me to say at that hour, roused out of a deep sleep. I had to refuse the call. I had given my pledge of silence to the Curtis board, as had my opponent. I kept my pledge, but my opponent shrewdly leaked the information through a third party.

When my wife said I was unavailable, the reporter told her that his story would report the next day that I had been charged with mismanagement. (Whether that reporter later found it possible to use that one telephone call to claim fairness and objectivity, I do not know.)

The kind of fear I experienced from this was new to me. It was not physical, and in this case I was not alone. I had a wife, four children, relatives, friends—all of whom could be hurt by this story.

I couldn't get back to sleep. I had to wait, like a condemned man, until 8 a.m., when I could get the newspaper. There, on the front page under a picture, was the story. My reaction was totally unlike the reaction to physical fear, which is spontaneous. This crept over me slowly. That quarter-hour, reading and rereading the story, was the worst in my life since the war. It wasn't until I did a quick review of my good fortune—I was alive, I had four healthy children, a lot of friends (my subsequent troubles thinned out that crowd), a contract which made me economically secure, and a naive faith in the press and the fairness of most business people. I knew I could handle conscious fear reasonably well, but this deep, internal—almost subconscious—kind was new to me, and initially unmanageable.

I was able to get to sleep each night with relative ease, but somewhere between 3 and 4 a.m. an internal alarm would clang, and I'd be instantly awake, sweating and staring up at the ceiling. I couldn't get back to sleep, and in those long, dreary hours I worried about my future and that of my family.

This went on for almost a week, and it made me less effective in handling my daytime problems, which burgeoned after the *Times* story. And the stories didn't stop. At the newspaper's urging, the reporter covered it every day for about two weeks, using colorful, extravagant terminology, in sorry contrast to the calm, businesslike coverage of the *Wall Street Journal, Newsweek,* and *Advertising Age.*

Despite the firing of my attackers and my vindication by the investigating committee of the board, the *New York Times*'s treatment during the first few days prevailed. Other reporters, very impressed by the *New York Times*, picked up this jaundiced theme and did irreparable damage to my reputation as an overall administrator. Fortunately, no damage could be done to my reputation as a trouble-shooting, top marketing executive, which even the hostile *Time* magazine business department called "unshakable."

I knew I had to do something about the subconscious alarm that was wrecking my sleep. I wouldn't use drugs, so I tried exhausting myself with exercise, sauna baths, and massage. It worked partially. Instead of awakening at 3 a.m., I'd sleep soundly till around 5. Most important, I decided not to stay in bed after awakening. I'd get up, shadowbox for ten minutes, take a blazing hot, then shockingly cold, shower, and start writing. The program was a therapeutic wonder.

All of these experiences went into my mental computer for developing a technique for mastering fear. I found supplementary aids, such as music, spy adventure novels, and exciting movies, to be good tension relievers as well. At a dinner party for an 80-year-old friend I got another point of view, when he read a poem by an anonymous philosopher, which concluded with the lines:

> When I get up in the morning,
> I read the obituary column—
> If I don't see my name, I'm happy for the day.

There have been other more recent incidents that held a potential for fear for me.

In December 1968, when the press was describing Saigon as a civil war battleground, I rode in a pedicab through the streets of the city. My heart pounded, my skin crawled, but I refused to be immobilized by fear.

Later, with the help of General Westmoreland, commander in chief of our forces in Vietnam, I flew in a helicopter to Battle Zone Two, north of Saigon, for a visit with my World War II outfit, the First Infantry Division. Flying over the jungle, known to contain enemy soldiers, and later on the ground, I was nervous, charged up, worried, but not afraid.

In 1969 I flew the equivalent of twice around the world. On one leg of this journey, the jet I was aboard was well down the runway when a fire warning light flashed on the instrument panel. The pilot instantly decided not to take off. The plane raced perilously down the runway, off the runway, and into an open field, bumping, grinding, swerving all the way. The plane finally slowed down and stopped without damage or fire. I was very concerned, but I remained calm.

In everybody's life there are situations that cause fear. What we must learn to do is to handle these situations in a physically and mentally constructive way. Remember the line from Shakespeare: "Cowards die many times before their deaths, the valiant never taste of death but once." To which I might add that those many deaths are agonizing and that one is mercifully quick.

Problems are only dangerous when they are not dealt with. Inaction and brooding are the absolute worst. Heavy physical exercise and mental diversion (movies, reading, romance, conversation) can be lifesavers in times of stress.

Don't be panicked by threats, particularly threats of legal action. Most threats are not carried out; most complaints never get into court.

The hardest worry to rout concerns loved ones and friends. Do what you can to solve the problem, so your conscience will be clear. And remember the therapeutic value of activity.

My final advice: When you think you've reached your breaking point, jump in a lake, river, ocean, or pool. Swim! I'm sure there are deep historical, physical, metaphysical, and physiological reasons for the therapeutic value of total immersion, but one jump into cool water and a few laps, even dog paddling, is near miraculous. If you can't swim, get into a steam room or sauna bath. Do both, swim and sweat, if you can. You may prevent a breakdown or stress-related physical disorder. In general, follow these simple rules:

1. Only the dead, very young, and unborn have no major problems. Life is filled with them, so you must be philosophical. Hope for the best, plan for the worst, and take what comes with humor and style. Remember, it is in troubled times that we grow the most.

2. Don't whine. Sooner or later most of us will get pretty much what we deserve. So try to deserve the important things in life: love, respect, friendship, responsibility, tranquility (but the last only when you are old).

3. Only rarely will anything turn out as badly as you fear it will. So why waste the time it takes to imagine the worst? Give yourself a break.

4. When trouble does come, don't give in to first inclinations to immobility and solitude. They are both to be avoided. Get out; get away, if you can. Keep very active. See all the friends and acquaintances you can. Tell your troubles to trusted friends, clergymen, doctors, lawyers. Increase your sexual activity if possible, and under no circumstances decrease it, whatever its rate. Stress can

"turn you off" very effectively, if you let it. Long-term detrimental effects can result if you stop or drastically cut down sexual activity.

5. If your sleep is badly affected, cut down on your evening meal, and start doing evening exercises. The ideal way to eat during stressful times is a large breakfast, a light lunch, and very little dinner. Listen to music; read exciting escape fiction.

6. Don't drink to drown your sorrows. That way out is cowardly and foolish. It will deepen your problems, reduce your fighting ability, and hurt your family and friends.

7. Help others. This may be the best advice I can give you. There is something spiritual, uplifting in helping others. You'll see your own problems in better perspective when you've been exposed to those of others. During that air lift discussed earlier, seeing others who had been more seriously hurt than I helped me to count my blessings.

8. Never despair, never give up.

There you have my "formula" for overcoming fear. It worked for me; it can, with variations, work for you.

4.
Distress and the Onset of Disease

Keith Sedlacek, M.D.

The fear of dying in warfare provides one of the most easily understood instances of the flight or fight response. The mind, realistically perceiving the threat to life and limb, acts accordingly. The cortex sends its messages to the limbic system to go into "red alert." This causes the hypothalamus and the pituitary to dramatically increase their output.

The hypothalamus and the pituitary are the areas in the limbic system that are primarily responsible for the hormone level in the blood. The hypothalamus sits directly over, and is in direct chemical and physical linkage to, the pituitary. The pituitary, called the "master gland" of the body, activates and controls, through feedback loops, the amount of hormones circulating. This pituitary-adrenal axis is what Dr. Selye discussed in his general adaptation syndrome.

When the fight or flight response is activated, the hypothalamus sends signals to increase the sympathetic outflow, causing an increase in epinephrine (adrenalin) and norepinephrine (noradrenalin). (These chemicals are also referred to as the catecholamines.) This intense response will also cause the hypothalamus to activate the pituitary to higher output so that other hormones, such as growth hormones, are increased. As these hormones and other chemicals circulate in the blood, they activate the sexual organs, the thyroid, and the pancreas, which in turn produce their hormones. Soon greater levels of catecholamines, and the hormones—cortisol, growth hormone, testosterone, thyroxine, and insulin—are flowing through the body. The whole body, now bathed in chemicals, is at its peak strength and is ready to defend itself or flee (rapidly).

As Joe Culligan pointed out, his twelve-hour ordeal in Belgium was terrifying. His body was bathed in chemicals because of the strongly activated fight or flight response; he described the cold sweat, the fear, and his attempt to control it, by recognizing that any bullet he heard was one that had not hit him. You can see how exposure to such stress day after day, month after month, and in some cases year after year, could cause "shell shock" or "war neurosis." Under these conditions, men may break under the pressure and run, or become so disabled emotionally and physically that they have to be removed from duty and hospitalized. Unless they are treated soon after the experience, they may remain sick or "shellshocked" for the rest of their lives.

Joe suffered a severe wound, and it was those stress-activated hormones that helped him to make the trip to the medic (plus, as he mentioned, good planning that made medical aid easily accessible to the wounded). It is when excessive levels of hormones are sustained without respite that the possibility of onset of such ailments as hypertension, peptic ulcers, and accelerated heart disease is increased.

Joe withstood the loss of his eye, but still had to go through the attack on the plane that was evacuating him. Instinctively he realized the often devastating effects of being immobilized and helpless. Joe's ability to assist those injured soldiers who were strapped down helped him to reduce his own fear. His activity served as a distraction.

Activity is generally recommended during times of stress, although certain kinds of activity, for example, what psychiatrists call "acting out," do not deal with the situation and can be inappropriate and destructive. Activity in a real situation, whether dealing directly or indirectly with the stress, has a number of beneficial effects. First, through it we may discharge the energy or arousal that was generated by the flight or fight response. Second, it may divert our attention. Third, it can give us a feeling of mastery and control regardless of the result. Finally, directed activity may change or influence the actual stressor or the conditions that created the stress (such as in the reduction of pollutants).*

Experiments done on people who were deprived of sensory information (stressors) and who were limited in their movement have shown that disorganization, hallucination, and even psychosis can result. Dr. Jay Weiss at Rockefeller University performed an experiment dealing with the notion that helplessness is also a major factor in the formation of peptic ulcers under stress. In one condition of the experiment, a rat could avoid an electric shock by pressing a bar with its head.

The other rat was "yoked" to the first rat (i.e., he received the same amount of shock as the first rat). He was helpless to change or stop the shock and entirely dependent on the first rat's ability to

---

*R. Gal and R. Lazarus, "The Role of Activity in Stress," *Journal of Human Stress*, December 1975.

avoid the shocks. The helpless rat developed severe
stomach ulceration, whereas the rat that could take
some action escaped the severe ulceration. This experiment showed that lack of control and a feeling of
helplessness may cause a continual state of fear and
anxiety which can bring about severe ulcers. Dr.
George Engel of Rochester Medical School, com-
menting on Dr. Weiss's work, said that "the important variable was what the animal could do about
the shock." Indeed, studies that I am now doing
with hypertensive patients seem to confirm that
people who feel helpless in a situation appear to be
less able to maintain control of their blood pressure.

People who are passive or who have great difficulty in taking action in stress situations remain in
these states of anxiety longer. The ability to commu-
nicate your feelings and thoughts and to act on
them will help you to cope with stress and help to
keep you from reaching the breaking point.

In training my patients to deal more effectively
with stress, I encourage them to do specific exercises
and to note their physical and mental reactions.
Then, through the assistance of sophisticated biofeedback equipment, they can learn what is relaxing
and what is exciting to their bodies. Through experiencing this tension and relaxation, they can learn to
relax each day for two 15-minute periods. This program will be discussed more thoroughly in Chapter
Eleven, where some of the procedures for retraining
the autonomic (sympathetic and parasympathetic)
nervous system are described.

The armed forces have, naturally, had a great
deal of interest in how men deal with the stress of
battle. During World War II, they used psychiatric

testing to screen potential soldiers. They discovered later that some men who had been judged to be psychologically and physically healthy in civilian life, and thus good candidates for soldiers, were unable to perform military duties because of repressed conflicts that were reawakened in the military.

Of the individuals predisposed to break down (as predicted by the testing), only one in three actually did break down.* Psychiatrists learned that if a man knows that the period of stress has a limit, he can better withstand it.

Consequently, in the Korean War the armed services decided to establish a "Policy of Forward Treatment." This policy consisted of limited combat duty (from six to eight months), followed by rest and relaxation (R & R), and then a quick return to duty. The results were excellent. The hospital admission rate for psychiatric conditions, shown in Figure 2 (page 54), demonstrates how well the policy worked. The rates were lower in the Korean War than in World War II and declined further, as the armed forces continued to use this policy.

The policy worked because the men knew what they had to endure and that once it was over, they would get a period of rest.

There also was a decrease in the cases that were evacuated from the War Theater during the Korean War (see Table 1, page 54).

Approximately 75 percent fewer patients were evacuated from the Korean War for psychiatric rea-

---

*Group for the Advancement of Psychiatry, "Preventive Psychology in the Armed Forces, with Some Implications for Civilian Use," Report no. 47. GAP, Oct. 1960, 419 Park Avenue South, New York, N.Y. 10016.

FIGURE 2.   ADMISSION RATES FOR PSYCHIATRIC CONDITIONS,
BY YEAR, 1938-1958

ARMY ACTIVE DUTY PERSONNEL, WORLDWIDE

RATES EXPRESSED AS NUMBER OF ADMISSIONS PER YEAR PER 1,000 AVERAGE STRENGTH

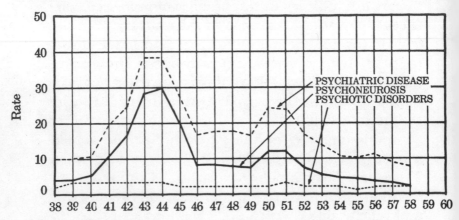

Source: Group for the Advancement of Psychiatry, "Preventive Psychology in the Armed Forces, with Some Implications for Civilian Use," Report no. 47, p. 290. GAP, Oct., 1960, 419 Park Avenue South, New York, N.Y. 10016.

Table 1
Percent of Total Evacuees That Were Psychiatric Cases, Japan-Korea (9/50–5/51) and Overseas Theaters, WW II (1944)

Theater	Period	Psychiatric Cases Evacuated Percent of Total Evacuees
All Overseas Theaters World War II	1944	22.99
European	1944	19.89
Mediterranean	1944	17.72
Southwest Pacific	1944	30.22
Japan-Korea	Sept. 1950– May 1951	6.29

Source: "Preventive Psychology in the Armed Forces," p. 290.

sons than during World War II. Also the men who returned to duty performed almost as well as other returnees to combat after hospitalization for other diseases or injuries, or absence for administrative reasons. Thus, due to a decrease in the stress period, fewer men reached their mental or physical breaking point.

The discharges for psychiatric disorders also fell (Figure 3), so that there was a decrease in the number of men lost to duty, and therefore a decrease in paperwork, and an increase in the self-confidence of men who were not evacuated. (If evacuated to the United States, many men remained in the "sick" or "injured" role.) These stress management steps appeared to help the military as a whole as well as the individual soldiers.

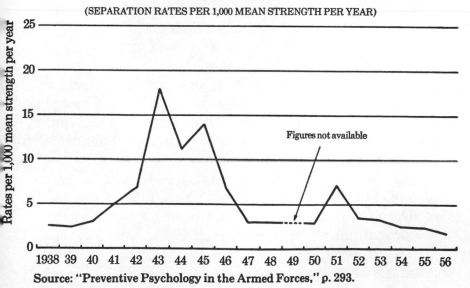

FIGURE 3.   SEPARATIONS FOR DISABILITY
DUE TO PSYCHIATRIC DISORDERS: U.S. ARMY
(1938-1956)
(SEPARATION RATES PER 1,000 MEAN STRENGTH PER YEAR)

Figures not available

Source: "Preventive Psychology in the Armed Forces," p. 293.

This same program of stress management was used by Peace Corps psychiatrists to help Peace Corps volunteers to maintain their psychic integrity. By studying the peak evacuation periods and instituting supportive programs, they dramatically reduced the Peace Corps rates of evacuation.

The Army and Peace Corps evaluated the stresses, noted the length of time their members could endure without breaking, and then introduced R & R or other preventive measures. At present I am involved in examining the possibilities of using this type of stress management program to reduce stress and dropout rates at a major law school.

Through the application of general principles of stress management, the health of these groups was maintained. I believe that we are now at the point where we can deliver training in stress management to the individual and offer important supportive measures for large groups of people.

But first we need to make people more aware of the damaging effects of stress. One way to do this is to predict which kinds of people seem headed for stress-related disease. The scale of Life Change Units (LCU), devised by Drs. Tom Holmes and Richard Rahe, can be used to indicate which categories of individuals these are.

This scale is simply a listing of forty-three different life events (such as marriage, retirement, the death of loved one, a job promotion), most of which occur in all our lives sooner or later, with a rating next to each indicating the relative upheaval (or stress) this event causes us. The higher a person scores on the scale (the more changes that are occurring in his or her life), the greater the chances of distress and disease.

Holmes and Rahe first tested this measurement on eighty residents of Seattle whom they followed for two years. The relative ratings for each of the life events were devised by the subjects. The ratings reflected their perception of how much stress these events caused in their lives. (If you look at Figure 4, you will note that the death of a spouse got the highest rating (100 points), marriage got a relatively high rating of 50, and Christmas was near the bottom with 12.) After two years, 86 percent of the subjects who scored over 300 points (over a one-year period) on the Life Change Scale experienced a major illness. Of those whose scores were between 150 and 300 points, 48 percent became ill, and 33 percent of those scoring less than 150 points experienced a change of health. (It is interesting that Joe scored 339 on the Holmes-Rahe scale in the six months that preceded his ulcer.)

In another study, the Holmes-Rahe scale was adapted for use with younger subjects and called the Social and Athletic Readjustment Scale. It was used to see if stressful events caused an increase in major injuries to college football players. An injury was defined as major if it caused the player to miss three practice sessions and/or one or more games. These were serious and often painful injuries.

The group was followed for two years. The players were divided by their scores on the scale into low-risk, moderate-risk, and high-risk groups. Thirty percent of the low-risk group, 50 percent of the moderate-risk group, and 73 percent of the high-risk group suffered major injuries. Note that some of the low-risk players received injuries and that not all of the high-risk players did. Thus while this study

FIGURE 4.
SOCIAL READJUSTMENT SCALE

Rank	Life Event	Mean Value
1	Death of spouse	100
2	Divorce	73
3	Marital separation	65
4	Jail term	63
5	Death of close family member	63
6	Personal injury or illness	53
7	Marriage	50
8	Fired at work	47
9	Marital reconciliation	45
10	Retirement	45
11	Change in health of family member	44
12	Pregnancy	40
13	Sex difficulties	39
14	Gain of new family member	39
15	Business readjustment	39
16	Change in financial state	38
17	Death of close friend	37
18	Change to different line of work	36
19	Change in number of arguments with spouse	35
20	Mortgage over $10,000	31
21	Foreclosure of mortgage or loan	30
22	Change in responsibilities at work	29
23	Son or daughter leaving home	29
24	Trouble with in-laws	29
25	Outstanding personal achievement	28
26	Wife begins or stops work	26
27	Begin or end school	26
28	Change in living conditions	25

29	Revision of personal habits	24
30	Trouble with boss	23
31	Change in work hours or conditions	20
32	Change in residence	20
33	Change in schools	20
34	Change in recreation	19
35	Change in church activities	19
36	Change in social activities	18
37	Mortgage or loan less than $10,000	17
38	Change in sleeping habits	16
39	Change in number of family get-togethers	15
40	Change in eating habits	15
41	Vacation	13
42	Christmas	12
43	Minor violations of the law	11

Source: T. Holmes and M. Masuda, "Psychosomatic Syndrome," *Psychology Today,* April 1972.

shows that those scoring high on the scale are more prone to injury, it does not designate the individuals who will actually be injured.*

It needs to be reemphasized that as with stress, the life events on the scale are not necessarily good or bad, they are simply times of extra strain. Marriage, for example, is thought of as a happy event. Yet we all know what stress the potential bride and groom are under. Before people marry, they often have doubts about themselves, their future partner, and the whole idea of marriage. A job promotion, no matter how much it has been sought, is also potentially a time of greater stress. It is entirely natural to

*S. Bramwell, M. Masuda, N. Wagner, and T. Holmes, "Psychosocial Factors in Athletic Injuries," *Journal of Human Stress,* June 1975.

experience some doubts about whether we can actually do the job, now that we've got it. When a couple are expecting their first child, it is often a time of great strain for both partners. We are all aware that we are under unusual stress when a loved one dies. But are we aware of the stress a change of residence will cause us? What we are suggesting here is that we simply must get in touch with our own feelings.

The scale can serve three functions for us. It can (1) tell us which life events cause extra stress; (2) help us realize why we are feeling stress; and (3) help us when we have choices (for instance, whether or not to take a new job) to regulate the amount of stress in our lives.

What all readers of this book should do now is to look at the scale and score themselves for the past year. If your score is over 150, and certainly if it is approaching or over 300, you may be predisposed to a stress-related disease. If you are experiencing symptoms of distress, it would be a good idea to see your doctor.

It is very important that we start getting in touch with our body and its reaction to stress. Take a few minutes and ask yourself these questions:

1. What are your goals in life? Are you sure you are not striving for more than you really want or need?

2. Are you leading your life your way? Or are you trying to measure up to someone else's (society's, the company you work for, or the neighbor's) standards?

3. Do you set aside time to relax and refresh your mind and body? Do you allow yourself enough

pleasure and rest? Or do you drive and push yourself constantly?

4. Are you maintaining healthy patterns of dealing with stress?

Clearly, we must each come up with our own answers to these questions. As individuals we have different needs and differing abilities to adjust to life. However, if we want a greater share of happiness from life, we would do well to honestly examine our life patterns and to adjust them accordingly to allow ourselves more room to relax, reflect, and become more responsible for all our activities.

5.
Personality Types That Seem More Susceptible to Stress-related Disease

Keith Sedlacek, M.D.

As more research is done in the field of medicine and psychiatry, it becomes increasingly clear that certain people by the nature of their behavior or personality are more susceptible to stress-related disease.

In *Type A Behavior and Your Heart* (Fawcett, 1974) cardiologists Meyer Friedman and Ray H. Rosenman pointed up the importance personality patterns play in causing heart disease. The authors feel that it is not only diet, heredity, and smoking, but, primarily, the person's behavior pattern that decides whether or not he or she will be stricken.

Friedman and Rosenman diagnosed Type A (high-risk) behavior as excessive competitiveness, constant impatience and struggle with time, insecurity (needing to always remind oneself and others of one's past achievements), aggressiveness and free-floating hostility, and a concern about numbers (liking to count possessions or accomplishments). They estimated that up to 50 percent of the U.S. population falls into this category (40 percent are Type B, and 10 percent have traits of both).

In a study in which 3500 men (over 35 and under 60 years old) were followed for a ten-year period commencing in 1960-1961, Dr. Friedman found that the Type A men had three times the incidence of coronary heart disease as Type B men. The doctors were so convinced by their findings that they stated in capital letters on the first page of their book: "In the absence of Type A behavior pattern, coronary heart disease almost never occurs before seventy years of age, regardless of the fatty foods eaten, the cigarettes smoked, or the lack of exercise. But when this behavior pattern is present, coronary heart disease can easily erupt in the thirties or forties."

This information helps explain why 28-year-old Detroit Lion football receiver Chuck Hughes collapsed and died of a heart attack after having caught a pass for a touchdown. A blood clot lodged in a severely diseased coronary artery killed him in front of 80,000 people in October, 1971.

As you can see, the traits of the Type A individual are almost all behaviors that trigger the flight or fight response. Consequently the Type A person is constantly in a state in which the sympathetic flow is supplying an excessive amount of cathecholamines (the chemicals activated when we are under stress), causing (1) an increased level of blood cholesterol, (2) a decreased ability to clear the blood of this cholesterol, (3) a prediabetic state, and (4) an increased tendency for the platelets and fibrinogen (the clotting elements of the blood) to fall out and settle onto the walls of the veins and arteries. As the veins and arteries become clogged, the heart has to work harder and harder to circulate blood throughout the body. Eventually the arteries will become so clogged that the heart will fail.

Concluding that the most lethal destroyer of the heart's arteries is the physical effects brought on by the presence of chronic Type A behavior, Friedman and Rosenman stated: "Rarely have we ever witnessed the onset of this disease in a person whose rate of manufacture and secretion of cathecholamines we did not know or suspect to have been increased."

These two cardiologists do not ignore the "probable causes" of heart disease: diet (cholesterol, fats, etc.), cigarette smoking, physical activity, heredity, obesity; nor do they minimize the "sure causes" of heart disease that demand continuous and regular supervision by a physician: diabetes, hypertension, hereditary hypercholesterolemia, and hyperthyroidism.

What Friedman and Rosenman are trying to impress on people is that healthy personality and behavior patterns are vital to a healthy heart. To prove this point, they did a six-month (January to June) study on a group of accountants. As the tax deadline approached in mid-April and greater time pressures overtook them, the accountants' level of serum cholesterol rose. A month or so later when the pressure was off, their cholesterol level fell. The authors state that "this change in serum cholesterol, then, could only have been due to their emotional stress—because neither their food, smoking, nor exercise habits had changed during the period of our surveillance."

This powerful influence of the emotions comes as no surprise to psychiatrists, who have long felt that a great many illnesses, particularly psychosomatic diseases, are caused by behavior patterns, or, as we call the more serious neurotic disturbances, personality disorders. The obsessive personality first described by Freud has many of the same traits as the Type A individual.

Freud suggested that early bowel training plays a particularly important role in the development of people who are competitive, excessively clean and orderly, submissive and driven. It is believed that very early bowel training (at 10 to 12 months) worsens this behavior pattern. The more humane practice is to start the training at 16 to 18 months, when the anal muscles are more fully developed and the child can more easily learn to control them. Everybody—the child, the parents, and society—gains from later training in that there are fewer hostile, obsessive individuals. Dr. Spock's suggestion for "later" bowel training may be the reason why our younger generation is less concerned about cleanliness and drive. It remains to be seen whether the younger generation's tendency to have less compulsive behavior patterns will result in fewer of them developing Type A personalities.

Freud also implied that men were often more obsessive, while women tended to be more hysterical. Today these differences based on sex appear to be diminishing as the attitude of the individual and society toward sex roles changes.

Up to this point we have been talking primarily about men and stress. Now it is time to examine the effects of stress on women.

It seems likely that women as they take more pressure-filled positions will fall prey to some of the stress-related diseases that previously struck mainly men. Dr. Marianne Frankenhaeuser, professor and dean of the Experimental Psychology Research Unit of the Swedish Medical Research Council, states that psychological and psychosocial stress conditions seem to suggest that the adrenal-medullary system is less reactive in females. She feels that women do not "show the same readiness as males to respond to environmental demands by adrenaline release." She believes that this response is due not to sex but to "a behavior pattern that is common to males in Western society."*

She continues that the "current change in sex-role patterns will lead to a growing proportion of Type A women, and an increase in susceptibility to diseases associated with the action of peripheral cathecholamines."

Friedman and Rosenman support this hypothesis in reporting that "the average blood cholesterol level our Type A women had was even higher than that of our Type A man." They also noted that in Japan since World War II the incidence of coronary heart disease among women has quadrupled as women have moved out of the home and into the job market.

I don't think any more evidence has to be presented that our behavior pattern has a great deal to do with the amount of distress we face. The problem now is to recognize what our individual disabling patterns are and to begin changing them before they destroy our bodies.

Let us look at the stress-related disease of hypertension (high blood pressure) and see what it would mean in terms of lives and happiness if we could control it. It is estimated that 15 to 30 percent (23 to 44 million people) of the adult population of

---

*M. Frankenhaeuser, "Women and Men Said to Differ in Their Response to Stress," *Psychiatric News,* June 18, 1975, p. 11.

the United States suffers from hypertension. It is a main if not major factor in heart attack and strokes, diseases that can cause irreversible brain and heart damage and that account for more than 50 percent of the deaths in the United States each year. †

The main way of treating hypertension is through medication that the patients must take three times a day for the rest of their lives. Most sufferers find this approach burdensome, and the control of hypertension has often been unsuccessful for lack of patients' compliance in taking medication.

But through public programs that offer free blood pressure tests, a start has been made to identify at least those with a high risk of hypertension. And the remedies for it are there if we can enlist the cooperation of the patients. One successful program was run at Gimbels department store. All the employees were tested at work, and it was discovered that 18 percent were hypertensive. Through the union they were offered drug treatment at the store.

I would suggest, however, that for as many as 60 percent of people suffering from labile and essential hypertension, there is a better way. Through biofeedback and perhaps one or two other methods, hypertensive people are learning voluntary control of their own blood pressure. The implications of this are enormous. Those who successfully learn to regulate their blood pressure will not only be taking on the responsibility for their health, but will be less dependent on medication and our health care system. The unsuccessful cases can return to the old treatment, having lost nothing.

---

†H. Benson, "Your Innate Asset for Combating Stress," *Harvard Business Review,* July-August 1974, p. 52.

The implications become even greater when people realize the large part *they* play in regulating their own disease and distress. With a coping device such as biofeedback, they are able to experience a greater sense of physical and mental well-being that may encourage them to give up destructive habits such as smoking. The threat of a stroke, lung cancer, or a heart attack sometime in the future has done little to stop life-long patterns of improper diet, lack of exercise, smoking, and general abuse of the body. But if individuals can see immediate results through their own efforts in the lessening or disappearance of their physical symptoms, they will usually feel encouraged to make more changes for the better.

Now that food and shelter are no longer the major concern of most Americans, it is time for us to recognize and deal with the stress in our lives. We can take action to lessen the outside factors such as pollution, noise, and time management. What we must also learn to work on is our internal environment. We must learn to better maintain and regulate the fluids that bathe every cell of our bodies. Dr. W. B. Cannon suggested we call the maintenance of a balanced internal fluid matrix *homeostasis*. Homeostasis is controlled by the two parts of the autonomic nervous system: the sympathetic and the parasympathetic. As you will recall, when triggered, the sympathetic part of the autonomic nervous system activates the chemicals we need in an aroused or excited state. The parasympathetic pathway, which is responsible for slower functions, essentially conserves and restores energy by slower rates of metabolism. Cannon stated that even with the great protective range of this balanced sympathetic-para-sympathetic system, if stress becomes excessive or critical, it could induce a breaking strain in the homeostatic mechanism.

Thus, by studying the critical stresses, we can obtain information regarding habits and practices that alter, *favorably or unfavorably,* the homeostatic mechanism. Cannon discovered, for example, that "during a cold, or after a recent illness, or when the body has been damaged by unhygienic living, or weakened by inactivity or by worry or dissipation or loss of sleep, the capacity for endurance is apt to be reduced."*

In a test of the effects of oxygen deficiency, Cannon placed a man in a test chamber at an elevation of 22,000 feet for fifteen minutes. The man experienced few physical or mental effects. That evening the man dined with friends, drank alcohol, and got to bed late. He awoke with a headache and a feeling of giddiness. When tested again, at 18,000 feet, he became dizzy and needed immediate administration of oxygen to keep him from fainting.

It seems clear that our physiological system has a great range of adaptability, but beyond a certain point, different for each person, changes in external conditions will necessitate greater alterations that will tax the body to its utmost capacity.

Let us look at one stress-related disease, migraine headaches, and see how it affects our homeostasis. Migraine headaches tend to run in families, and often there is also a family history of other

---

*W.B. Cannon, "Stresses and Strains of Homeostasis," *American Journal of the Medical Sciences*, January 1935, p. 10.

stress-related diseases, such as epilepsy (10 percent), allergies (30 percent), arthritis (29 percent), hypertension (60 percent), cerebral vascular accident (40 percent), and nervous breakdown (34 percent). Dr. H. Wolff has also reported that those prone to migraines demonstrate a characteristic personality profile; they are rigid, success-oriented, perfectionistic, conventional, and intolerant—in general, the obsessive-compulsive type.† There are also certain food substances that may trigger migraine attacks. These substances are listed in the Appendix.

There often are prodromal symptoms (warning events), before a migraine appears. These include an increased sense of well-being, excessive talkativeness, high spirits, unwillingness to retire, and increased appetite. *Immediately* before the onset there may be a sense of an impending attack, an increase in tension, hunger, visual defects (such as scintillating scotoma), vertigo, depression, or excessive sleepiness. The attack develops in two stages: first there is a constriction of the cranial vessels and then a swelling and throbbing of the external arteries, particularly the temporal artery. It is this second stage that causes the severe pain, and most people refer to this stage as the migraine headache.

The most common treatment is administration of an ergot compound, which if taken early enough, should stop or slow the headache. The medication acts to constrict the arteries, thus stopping this second painful stage, Dr. Wolff, who suffered from mi-

---

†H. Wolff, *Wolff's Headache and Other Head Pain.* 3rd ed., rev. by D. Dalessio. New York, Oxford Press, 1972, p. 294.

graine attacks, points out that tension appears to evoke the most intense headaches. These often occur before major life changes.

This painful affliction affects thousands of people. Usually they take powerful drugs (which must be limited because of their side effects), or they suffer stoically. There is frequently a genetic factor at work here: an inherited tendency toward vasoconstriction that can be triggered by stress. The body apparently overcompensates for this constriction by a dilation (expansion), which brings about the swelling and the painful headache.

In the past, drugs and psychotherapy have helped many people with migraines, but it appears that a new technology and therapy are now available to treat this stress-related disease—by teaching the sufferer how to vasodilate his or her arteries. This is done during the first stage of the headache, interrupting, lessening, or terminating the headache by correcting or overriding the tendency to constrict the arteries of the head. Control of the natural mechanism—constriction and dilation —rests in the hands of the patient, who no longer needs to rely on drugs.

Using prescribed daily mental and physical exercises, we can train the person to override consciously vascular constriction, and to keep the stress from reaching a critical triggering level. In terms of the autonomic nervous system, we "rebalance" the autonomic system toward a lesser sympathetic outflow. This voluntarily reduced outflow lessens the probability of the constriction of the arteries and thus the headaches. After sufficient therapy and practice, the patient can voluntarily vasodilate in a very short time, sufficient to stop or lessen the migraine attack.

In many ways this is similar to what psychotherapists do: they help patients to develop more conscious control over their actions; we help patients develop more conscious control over their mental and bodily reactions. In biofeedback we take physiological information gained from the machinery and feed it back to the patient, as well as using whatever verbal information and feedback the patient has to offer. Thus patients try first to gain control over these devastating physical symptoms; they can then continue in therapy to work on their other emotional problems. (For example, migraine sufferers often have problems of obsessiveness in their personal relationships.) It is possible to teach migraine patients control in two to seven practice sessions daily in a one-week or two-week program. More than a hundred patients have been treated in this manner, with an 82 percent success rate.*

For many people biofeedback appears to be a better starting point than psychotherapy for dealing with psychosomatic problems, because patients often experience these as physical problems and not as mental ones. Thus patients are often more willing to work on the physiological symptoms and can thereby learn more healthy self-regulation. Later they may be able to see that their emotional state also needs to be dealt with by means of some sort of further work. This could take the form of professional therapy, or the patient, who is now more healthily

---

*For a fascinating personal account of how biofeedback dispelled one person's painful migraine headaches, read Gerald Green, "How I Licked Migraine Headaches," *Family Circle*, February 2, 1976.

organized and regulated internally, can use his greater energy and patience to begin dealing with the external stressors himself. Without this healthy physiology, we are more prone to the disabling effects of outside forces.

Life is constant change and we continue to grow and develop, through childhood and adolescence, to adulthood. Each stage presents us with certain stresses and milestones that are necessary for our continued growth and health. A stable internal environment with a wide range of reactions from relaxation to fight or flight is absolutely necessary for the optimal opportunity to cope successfully with life. This has been pointed out by Dr. Hans Selye, who said that there are two kinds of adaptability: a superficial, readily available, replaceable type, and another more deeply hidden in reserve, which can replenish the superficial kind only after some rest or diversion. It is these deeper reserves that we talk about when we speak of homeostasis. The body seems to need a quiet time or a period dominated by the parasympathetic outflow in order to refresh and replenish itself and to continue to function at its best. If this time is not provided, the body wears down, and, finally, if run hard and long enough, death will result.

There seems to be a great deal of evidence that a person's behavior pattern is of prime importance in the efficient working of the autonomic system. It is thus necessary that we learn to evaluate and adapt to the particular external and internal conditions that affect each of us. We have touched on many of the probable causes of internal and external stress, and by now you may have thought of some from your own life. Why not take a sheet of paper and list the five major causes of stress in your life? In the next chapters we will not only tell you more about biofeedback, but we will describe some specific cases of stress-related diseases and offer some of the possible treatments for these and other stress-related diseases. Later in the book we will suggest specific home exercises and procedures that will help you to become aware of how you can best identify and deal with stress.

6.
Some Major Causes of Distress

Matthew J. Culligan

I have for decades objected to the "laundry list" approach of how-to books. The *New York Times* actually did print a list of the principal causes of negative strain or distress which, according to the doctors surveyed, drove 60 to 80 percent of their patients into their waiting rooms. The ailments they complained of were headaches, high blood pressure, pervasive anxiety, depression, pre-ulcer digestive problems, excessive drinking and smoking, and overweight.

The principal causes of these ailments as listed by the *Times* were death or the impending death of a loved one, serious illness, divorce or the breakup of an important relationship, despair or deep fear about children, loss of job, loss of home, relocation, and economic problems.

There can be no argument with this list or with the tragedies of psychosomatic illnesses stemming from these causes. But nowhere on the list was a factor that I feel is a primary cause of distress—time management.

THE MANAGEMENT OF TIME

I am certain that the failure of the average person to manage time is a major cause of distress and, therefore, is an underlying cause of psychosomatic illness. Happily, it is one cause of distress that can, if recognized, be corrected. Time, like money or any resource, can be managed.

Excellent work has been done on the management of time. Books and articles have been written on the subject and are available in your local library. My mission here is simply to develop your awareness of the fact that the race against time, every day of your life, can induce distress.

Sleeping half an hour less could be an immediate solution to the race against time. Starting earlier in the morning can help clear up a crowded schedule. (Of course, the first step might simply be to see if you're trying to accomplish too much. Constant time struggles usually indicate an overdeveloped drive to achieve.)

One of the most balanced, stress-resistant business leaders I have ever known *walked* to all of his appointments between 59th Street and 42nd Street in New York City. His faithful secretary calculated the walking time necessary, and she would alert him a minute before he should start walking. People needing to see him on an emergency basis could walk with him to his appointment. It was not an unusual sight to see my friend promenading uptown or downtown, east or west, being talked to, pleaded with, or gestured at by a companion wanting some favor or decision. My friend managed his time, but also managed to keep fit and relaxed while walking.

Start tomorrow, if humanly possible, to manage your time, as interpreted by your schedule. A well-ordered schedule is essential in the management of time. So is a method of handling telephone calls if the volume of calls is part of your problem.

I neither make nor take telephone calls between 9 a.m. and 11 a.m. But then I do nothing but make, take, and return calls from 11 a.m. to 12:15 p.m. The volume of uninterrupted work that can be done using this method is extraordinary. Trying to do both—work and take calls—is time-wasting, distracting, and tension-inducing.

IMPATIENCE

Impatience doesn't show up on any list of seven deadly sins or as a specific medical term related to psychosomatic illness. But, as my antennae have broadened their scope, I have noticed increasingly the look of distress on the faces of people waiting impatiently at red lights, bus stops, theater lines, elevators, and retail counters. One bank on 42nd Street in New York City has actually posted guards to keep irate customers from repeating physical assaults on bank tellers.

Impatience is a little rage which, if it lasts long enough, can send those signals described by Dr. Sedlacek throughout the body. They can help bring on psychosomatic disorders.

This kind of distress can be transformed into positive energy in several ways. I carry a book or magazine with me, and if I must wait, I read. If the lighting is bad, I do stomach exercises. I pull in my stomach and hold it in for three to five seconds, let it out, and repeat the process while I wait. Isometric exercises can also be done while standing in one spot. If people around you think you are strange or afflicted, just smile.

For salespeople, waiting time can be used to

write memos and reports. A rather special gimmick is used by a friend of mine. He whips out a pocket calculator and has a lovely time computing while he waits.

My daughter has supplied several constructive and healthy ways to endure waiting time. In buses she does needlepoint; in cars (with the windows closed, since she has a voice like a sick bullfrog) she sings at the top of her lungs, either with or without the radio; in bank lines and waiting for elevators, she has been known to have actually *talked* to the other people on line! There are many ways to ease anxiety while waiting, and even the simplest things, such as daydreaming or thinking about a good evening last week can turn a potentially stressful time into quite a pleasant one.

My earlier education and training in writing and reporting give me a huge advantage. I can write almost any place, and I do—in reception rooms, taxis, restaurants (much of this book was written at long breakfasts at the famed Algonquin Hotel in New York City), on trains, and on planes.

Those trained in TM (transcendental meditation), EST (Erhard Seminars Training), and General Semantics often meditate while waiting. They eliminate distress and actually refresh themselves with brief meditation exercises. Eastern people often carry worry beads, polished stones that they hold and rub to eliminate tension while they wait.

Pocket transistor radios, particularly those with ear plugs, are handy companions while waiting for almost anything. Beautiful, relaxing, or stirring music can melt away distress.

The pattern, you will notice, is completely consistent. *Action*—physical, emotional, and/or mental—is an antidote for distress.

INCREASED FREQUENCY AND PACE OF CHANGE

The rapidity of change in the modern world is undoubtedly a new factor to be added to the list of distress causes. Over the last thirty years we have developed atomic bombs, television, jet planes, tranquilizers, and space flights, to name only a few of the innovations that are changing all of our lives. These major changes in the speed of travel and events have tended to increase stress-related symptoms and diseases.

The atomic bomb has placed a tremendous threat over each of us and the world itself. The picture of the spreading mushroom cloud and the destruction of the people and cities of Hiroshima and Nagasaki has been fixed in every person's consciousness or preconsciousness. The pressure of the threat of destruction of all life on this earth has created a "live for the moment" ethic that has a synergistic relationship with the sexual revolution and the drug culture.

All this has continued and accelerated the deterioration of the "extended" family. More people today are facing life alone with a greater sense of their individual vulnerability, as well as that of the world's.

The invention of TV was a big jump from radio. Now people and events from all over the world can be seen and heard in our own living rooms. With TV satellites we now have a worldwide visual communication system, making the world smaller and every part of it more accessible. In addition to the obvious benefits of this system, we are able to view the distress of world disease and starvation and the devastation of war. The effect on the nervous systems of adults and children who watch these events and conditions on TV is as yet unknown, but we do know that children and adults now spend large amounts of time in front of the TV set. It has been suggested that there is a correlation between the violence witnessed on TV and the increase in crime on the streets. This has not yet been proven, but an increasing number of thoughtful observers are pondering this link.

Jet travel has done an enormous amount to make the world smaller. By commercial flight we can now go halfway around the world in fourteen to sixteen hours (New York to Australia, for example). Such rapid travel has also created the stress-related illness called "jet lag," which is probably caused by the stress of travel and perhaps by the effect on the body of different gravitational forces.

Along with the introduction of antibiotics, one of the major recent contributions of medicine has been the use of the tranquilizers and antipsychotic medications. Since the late 1950s these drugs have helped doctors deal with a great range of severely disturbed behavior. Before the advent of these medications, patients in mental hospitals were hosed down when they had become so agitated that they could not be bathed. Instead of using strait jackets and hoses, we can now give pills or injections. There are drawbacks to these drugs—drowsiness and lethargy—but the overall benefit has been enormous.

Inevitably, drug use expanded beyond the institutions and into our daily life. Milder tranquilizers were introduced as a reliever of everyday anxiety and minor pain. Indeed, because it was easier to eliminate the symptom than to deal with its cause, tranquilizers came to be prescribed more and more by doctors and demanded more and more by patients. (People often feel that they are not being actively treated if the doctor does not give them a prescription or an injection.) In 1964, 45 million prescriptions were written for antianxiety drugs. By 1970 more than 80 million prescriptions were being written annually, mainly for the tranquilizers Valium and Librium, making them among the most prescribed drugs in the United States.*

Another area in which disturbing changes are taking place is in the processing of food. More and more artificial preservatives and additives are being introduced into packaged foodstuffs. Many of these chemicals, and their quantities, do not have to be shown on the packaging label.

Increasingly it is believed that some of these substances are causative factors in disease and disorder. Some research has been done connecting hyperactivity in children to these chemicals, and it is also now being shown that migraine headaches can be triggered by chemical substances. In view of the fact that we don't know the effects of these chemicals, I feel that these substances should be thoroughly tested for their safety before being added

---

*"Patients Still Are Seeking Emotional Help Within Medical Model," *Clinical Psychiatric News*, vol. 3, no. 9, September 1975, p. 17.

to our food. Isn't our nation's health more important than shelf life?

Space travel represents the area of greatest potential for future change. We can already place men on the moon, and we soon will be exploring the more remote planets. There are now proposals for self-sustaining space stations. In 1960 these were dreams that were written about only in science fiction novels. As they become reality, the technology used in these missions is bound to inject changes into our everyday existence, giving us more to deal with and adjust to.

The point of these examples is to show how rapidly change is coming at us. Change creates new stresses to which we must adapt. With these changes, the proliferation of choice, greater mobility, and the decrease of the extended family, the individual is being asked to adjust to more and to do it more rapidly.

LIGHTING AND NOISE

Two further potential stressors of modern life are improper lighting and noise. It wasn't until 1963 that I realized the distress that could be caused by poor lighting. In that year as chief executive officer of the Curtis Publishing Company, I was responsible not only for the well-known magazines but for Curtis's gigantic understructure—vast timber holdings, paper mills, transportation systems, printing plants, and distribution companies.

Curtis, as I have said, was hard pressed to survive, having been mismanaged for decades. Practically in the middle of an agonizing budget crisis, the chief financial officer gave us the shocking news that our major insurance company was going to raise our insurance rates because of a sharp increase in accidents in Curtis plants. This increase compared unfavorably not only to Curtis's past history, but also to industry averages.

I pleaded with the head of the insurance company (fortunately a golf partner) for six months to be allowed to correct the problems (mental note: if I could find them). He agreed; so I directed two industrial engineers to undertake a crash program of research. The first pass didn't tell enough. Accidents were more frequent in all plants, but no common denominator was evident. I asked for an accident count by periods of the day—morning, afternoon, and evening—and by days of the week. The answer literally leapt out of the statistics. There were almost no accidents in the mornings of Tuesday, Wednesday, and Thursday; just a few on Monday mornings (we could attribute these to weekend excesses); and a few on Friday mornings (fatigue and preoccupation with the coming weekend). Most of the accidents occurred from the middle of the afternoon until quitting time. A lucky inquiry brought out the common denominator. In an economy move, the plant *lighting* had been reduced. Working all day in inadequate or barely adequate light was causing visual discomfort in many and visual disability in others. We immediately readjusted the lighting, and within a week the medical department reports showed a sharp drop in accidents.

I was too busy to pursue the lighting problem any further at that time, but the incident went into my memory bank. It emerged years later when the first publicity appeared citing noise and pollution as causes of human distress; I added light to that equation.

As I studied the problem, I realized that there was more, much more, to the light situation than just intensity. The *quality* of light was equally important.

Cold cathode light is the illumination closest to bright sunlight. It is, obviously, the best light, but it does cause glare. Polaroid glasses reduce the glare, but they also cut down the light. Fluorescent lighting is commercially successful, but recent studies indicate that it is not beneficial to the people working in it. Many hours of exposure to this light, which flickers at a subliminal level, can have a negative psychological effect.

Lighting engineers and experts are working on variations of lighting techniques. Indirect lighting, diffused lighting, and color filters seem to hold promise.

The lighting problem, of course, is not restricted to workers in plants. Most offices and many board and conference rooms have overhead fluorescent light. The worst physical effect of poor lighting is visual discomfort, which should disappear with escape and rest. But the psychological "damage" is potentially much more serious. Headaches, bad temper, and other emotional disorders may result from hours spent in poor lighting.

The effects of noise on our bodies and minds are being studied throughout the world. It has, of course, been known for years that constant exposure to very loud noise can cause severe damage to our hearing and nervous systems. But increasingly it is felt that noise is a stress factor that can bring about widespread disturbances in various biochemical and physiological activities in the human body.*

THE MEDIA

Years ago, at the end of a week in which the world seemed to be in utter turmoil with unhappy, threatening events cascading upon it from a press competing for attention, I had the sudden thought that *stress* and *press* sound uncannily alike.

There is no inclination or attempt here to blame the messenger for the bad news, but the distress caused by the press in the United States is mountainous. The reporters, editors, headline writers, photographers, picture editors, and caption writers are solely motivated by the need to grab and hold our attention.

What can the individual do to relieve the tension caused by the press? Several things, the first of which is to understand the nature of the press. It is an aggregation of businesses seeking to make a profit out of circulation income and advertising. The advertising rate is based on circulation. Circulation is gained by sensationalism in headlines, text, and pictures.

Editorial writers and columnists and TV commentators need to get and hold our attention. So they must avoid the routine, dull affairs of daily life. They must always try to interest us, excite us, outrage us. Once we comprehend this, we can perhaps

---

*B. Welch and A. Welch, *Physiological Effects of Noise*. New York, Plenum Press, 1970.

pick up a newspaper or magazine or watch our favorite TV commentator with a tongue-in-cheek
skepticism, determined not to accept automatically
anything that is said, but to wait until the facts
emerge, as they generally will, in time.

When you've accomplished that, try this experiment. Don't read a newspaper, a news magazine, or
watch a television news show for one week. Instead
listen to music, or read, or watch your local educa-
tional TV network, whose shows, with the help of
our British cousins, are often quite wonderful.

Believe me, for I have done it often, the world
will not fall apart, and you will be freeing yourself
from this self-induced form of slavery to sensationalism.

AMBITION

Ambition can be acceptable, beautiful, or repugnant. The ambition to achieve good and great
objectives for money, power, prestige, security, and
privacy for self is quite acceptable in our society.
The ambition to achieve great objectives in worthwhile causes (Jean Monet, Albert Schweitzer, Dr.
Dooley) is a beautiful human trait. The ambition to
achieve money and power for reasons of dominance,
hedonistic self-gratification, false pride, or arro-
gance is distasteful and repugnant to most people.

One of the most powerful and despotic leaders
in American business was pleased to say: "I don't
get ulcers, I give them." His technique for retaining
control was to divide and conquer. He set executives
against each other, letting them spend themselves
in internecine battles, then he got rid of the strong-

est. His price for survival was unquestioning loyalty, not to the company but to himself personally.

Such individuals don't buy books like this one. They avoid distress by expending energy in programs good for the country, the company, the stockholders, and themselves—but in reverse order, despite the attempts of public relations experts to convince us otherwise. Hopefully, most readers of this book will have the first kind of ambition, and maybe a few the second kind. It is quite natural for intelligent, well-educated people to be ambitious, once they have observed the benefits of success.

There are problems, however, with this kind of striving. There is a tendency to become arrogant and insufferable as greater success and power are gained and to get out of touch with the needs of loved ones.

My case exemplified the typical New York– Westchester– Connecticut success syndrome. I was very ambitious, with the intellectual and physical attributes to get to the top. I did so four times, becoming chief executive officer of four companies by age 42.

In the process, however, my marriage broke up, and I lost contact with my four children. The marriage was irretrievable, but fortunately my children were tolerant and I was able to restore an excellent relationship with my son and oldest daughter, a fair one with my youngest daughter, and an armed truce with my middle daughter.

My heartfelt advice to the rationally ambitious is to be sure you are not working for wine when your spouses and children would prefer water.

Ambition for good causes is pure positive energy. Needy causes abound in business, society, and politics, which are desperately looking for this kind of energy.

CHILDREN

I would have been willing to put all the hours it would take to write this book into this section alone, but it would be vain and perhaps dangerous for me to do more than write my part of this chapter as a parent of four children, and the grandparent of an ethnic marvel whose forebears are Irish, English, Spanish, German, Ukranian, Russian, and Yugoslav.

Parents don't always or even often understand themselves as they mature. The same applies for children; so why should there be any surprises at failures of communication within families?

In the young there is always a very rapid, often immediate, reaction to any kind of stimulation. In adults, who usually have learned from life experiences, the reactions are slower, more controllable, and more controlled.

An extraordinary man, Angus (Gus) Lightfoot Walker, a giant in intellect, culture, and humanity, as well as physique, told me the following story. Gus had one son, with whom he was having some difficulty communicating. He was grieved and concerned by it, but because of his magnanimous spirit, he came to this conclusion: His son was 20, he was 63. Gus reasoned that he had been an adult for forty-three years, his son for two. He concluded that his advantage after forty-three years of life experience was towering. After only two years of adult ex-

perience, why *should,* how *could,* his son know what
Gus knew? In any other arena it would be absurd to
measure the performance of a human being with
two years of experience against that of a man with
over twenty times that much. After listening to Gus
Walker, I recalled the words of the philosopher who
said: The young do not know what older generations
know, which is nature's way of protecting creativity;
the older do not have the drives and passions of the
young, which is nature's way of enabling them to
survive.

If you have children in the dangerous years between 12 and 20, I urge your acceptance of the fact
that your relationship with your children for the
rest of your life starts in the next ten seconds.

I have only one message for all parents of children under 20. Give them all the love you are capable of giving, give them as much education as
they'll accept, and don't give up on them even in
their worst moments. If they threaten to leave, or do
leave, tell them you hate what they are doing, but
you love them, and that they can come back when
they are ready.

AGING

No one will dispute the distressing effects of aging on the body. But some measures can be taken to
lessen these effects and to prolong good health. I will
restrict myself here to observations about my own
technique. The need for a personal program became
apparent to me because I have known many older
men and been genuinely fond of and interested in
them. Too often I have observed the dramatic and

saddening changes that seemed to occur around the classic retirement age of 65. I tried to get below the surface of this phenomenon, which seemed to involve physical changes as well as psychological ones.

Older people are identifiable by the stiffness of their walk. I resolved to avoid that mark of old age by following a regimen of exercise that would keep my body supple and strong. I selected shadow boxing as a form of exercise, which I would do every morning for ten minutes. When I became bored with seeing my reflection on the wall while exercising, I took to doing my boxing in front of the TV, watching the "Today" show, in which I had been heavily involved while at NBC-TV. I box while I watch and listen, getting my exercise, news, weather, sports, and human interest stories at the same time.

I then related psycho-cybernetics to my desire to stay young in appearance and attitude. Up to that time, my forty-second year was the very best year of my life, with good health, prestige, and power in business; many good friends; no economic worries; and healthy kids. All seemed well with the world at that time. I decided to try to program my personal computer in such a way that I would always be 42 in spirit and attitude. I have refused to change my life style in terms of athletics, working hours, or enthusiasms. I have sought out young people (young in spirit, regardless of chronological age) as friends and acquaintances and have avoided people who think and act "old."

Once I reached the calendar age of 52 (though still 42 in spirit and attitude), I decided on specific programs to ward off some of the usual effects of aging.

I cut out drinking during the daylight hours because it made me drowsy in late afternoon. I practically eliminated meat from my diet because I felt that the chemical force-feeding of cattle might make meat dangerous. I started eating a good, well-balanced breakfast, a light lunch, and a tiny dinner three or more times a week. I drank only a vodka on the rocks before dinner and some wine during dinner.

I started walking after dinner, selecting a loop that took me past half a dozen theaters. When I'd spy a movie that looked interesting, I'd see it and then finish my leisurely walk home, having digested my meal quite thoroughly. My sleep has been deep and tranquil.

When I started to develop a slight potbelly, I increased my shadow boxing and I included several minutes of deep bending, hooking, jabbing, and uppercutting from a crouched position.

During my annual physical I asked my doctor about some veins on the right side of my left knee that seemed to have sprung during Ranger training. My internist referred me to my surgeon, who explained that those veins were losing their elasticity. The blood was not coursing through normally, and in the years ahead they could become troublesome and even inhibit some sports, particularly horseback riding. I opted for surgery, which could improve the condition. The operation on my left leg would eliminate the possibility of later distress due to a deterioration in my circulatory system. By having this operation, I made my left leg younger, in a practical sense, than it had been before the surgery. I increased my future capacity for enjoyment and good health by eliminating a block to a sport I dearly love, horseback riding.

On my next birthday I plan to undertake a weight reduction program. By reducing my top weight limit from 190 to 180 I will reduce the labor of my heart, make walking and swimming (as well as getting into a bathing suit) more pleasurable, and do wonders for my morale because I know my clothes will look better after the weight loss. I will continue to try to find new and different programs for reducing the penalties of aging where appearance, health, and vigor are concerned.

My programs for mental activity are already set. Writing books is a marvelous discipline for the mind. Research must be pursued, manuscript conferences and arguments with editors are stimulating, and there is great ego gratification in the evidence that my mind and imagination can create a "product" for which thousands of people are prepared to spend hard-earned dollars.

If I live into my seventies and eighties, I plan to go where life is the simplest. A place where a man can live in shorts and sneakers, fish, ride horses, swim, write, and argue with friends. I will try to identify more and more with my inner self, my spirit, soul, or whatever it is, and less with my physical side.

DEATH

I've encountered no serious argument to the proposition that the death of a loved one is the single most terrible experience in one's adult life. There is a wide range of emotional responses to death, which are largely dependent on the age of those who died and the age and condition of life of the survivors.

The death of a child or young adult can be the most devastating because the survivors mourn not only for the dead person but for themselves, because they have lost the opportunity to enjoy that person and to watch the progress and the growth that was to take place.

Death reminds us of how very alone we all are, and how critical love is to offset the desolation of continual loneliness.

My father died, in California, when I was 10 years old. He had been a remote figure to me, being an old-fashioned Irishman who really did believe children should be seen and not heard. His coffin was shipped back to us sealed, as was usual in those days. My older brother and sister grieved. They had gotten to appreciate him. My younger sister and I, though sobered by the loss of a parent, did not.

When my brother Ernest was killed in a skiing accident in the Alps above Salzburg, Austria, I grieved, somewhat for him but more for me because I wouldn't see him anymore.

A mutual friend sent me a sympathy card with a single sentence: "The game is done, I've won, I've won."

It was immediately comforting. My brother had had a full life. He had been a sportsman, a great competitor, and an inveterate ladies' man. I calculated that if he maintained his average of a new love every six months, he must have been happy with over a hundred beautiful women before the age of 50.

He had married and divorced three times and had managed to remain friendly with all three of his ex-wives. His last wife had been married to an important foreign diplomat, who at the time of his wife's romance with my brother challenged Ernest to a duel. Happily, she returned to her diplomat husband after her marriage to my brother broke up.

Ernest was also successful in business and had been an Undersecretary of the Interior in Washington, D.C., at 28. He had advanced rapidly in World War II, becoming military head of the Psychological Warfare branch in the Mediterranean.

Life to Ernest was an exciting game, and he had lived it to the fullest. Our friend was most perceptive. Ernest had played it his way and gone out in a dramatic finale.

My mother died at 78 of a massive cerebral hemorrhage. Her last action and words were a perfect example of the calm acceptance of death we all strive for.

My eldest sister, Marie, was sitting with my mother when she sighed, raised her hand to her forehead, started to make the sign of the cross, gasped "Jesus, Mary, and Joseph—help me!" Her hand fell, she collapsed sideways, unconscious, and slid into a coma from which, mercifully, she never recovered.

Marie heard the phrase, which my mother had probably repeated thousands of times in her lifetime. We were all calmly comforted by this account of the last seconds of my mother's conscious life. She didn't say "Call a doctor" or "Get an ambulance" when she knew something dreadful was happening to her. In the fraction of a second left to her consciousness, she put herself in the hands of her merciful God. Ever since that experience, I have pitied the elderly who do not have that God to rely on.

When a loved one dies, our immediate decision should be to turn the stress into positive energy, rather than to have it become distress. There are many details that must be attended to when a person dies. The doctor, if not in attendance at the time of death, must be notified immediately to complete a death certificate. The body must be removed by the mortician. Relatives and friends must be notified and comforted, and funeral arrangements started. These activities need positive energy—and will help to lessen the distress.

There are, of course, many more potential causes of distress in our lives. I have tried to isolate a few so that we can be more aware of their effects on us and of how we might begin to sidestep or adapt to these negative effects. It is clear so far that as a nation we have not done a good job in coping with these challenges. As I said earlier, it is estimated that from 60 to 80 percent of visits to doctors have to do with stress-related complaints.

Another disturbing sign is the increased dependence on drugs as a way of handling stress. By drugs, I mean not only marijuana, hashish, LSD, heroin, and amphetamines, but the so-called legal drugs, such as alcohol, tobacco, sedatives, and tranquilizers. Most of us have at one time or another turned to one of these substances to lighten or relieve stress, but increasingly people are becoming dependent or addicted to them. Alcohol, for example, is now the number one drug problem in the country, and more and more young people are turning to it.

Not only is this situation costly in business terms (absenteeism, accidents, inefficiency), but who can estimate the cost in terms of personal suffering and suffering inflicted on loved ones?

It is easy to blame and legislate against the suppliers: doctors, drug companies, and pushers, but it seems evident that the drugs are only a symptom of underlying problems. Because of the stress of modern life and the fragmentation of families and other social groups, the troubled individual looks for other gratification and for a way to dull the pain; drugs, which often bring about reduced awareness or unconsciousness of real life events and feelings, may temporarily provide the desired escape.

One of our purposes in this book is to suggest and provide alternate methods of evaluating and dealing with stress, so that there can be less dependence on these harmful substances. Only then will we be free to use our entire energy to deal with the problems at hand.

7.
What Is Biofeedback?

Keith Sedlacek, M.D.

From all the evidence presented thus far, I think everyone would agree that stress management is a desirable goal. Until recently, however, it was often difficult to know for certain when our bodies were reacting adversely to stress, unless we had a symptom or a disease. We could tell when our hands and armpits were sweating excessively or when our voice and body were quivering for no external reason, but how could we know when our blood pressure was rising or our skin temperature changing? What we needed was an accurate measuring device to tell us when we were distressed. That's where biofeedback came in.

Biofeedback is the monitoring of signals from the body, such as muscle tension and hand warmth, and the feeding of that information back through the use of sophisticated machines to the individuals so they can get external information as to exactly what's happening in their bodies. After the information is received, the patients are trained during a series of visits, ranging from six to twenty-five, depending on the symptom or ailment, to do certain exercises to relax the agitated part of the body. By the time treatment is finished, of course, patients are no longer dependent on the machine to supply information about their bodies.

Of course, the whole concept of body feedback is not new. Practically every learning situation in life is an example of this kind of feedback. If you have ever watched an infant trying to pick up a ball, you have seen feedback at work. The infant sees his arm and the ball, but somehow he can't get them to work together. By trial and error he slowly learns that he can move his arm in various ways. Eventually he incorporates that knowledge in the motor center of his cortex, and with fine adjustments he picks up the ball. He examines it and then may throw it. Later he repeats this whole adventure with obvious delight at the newly acquired skill that is his for life. The same process applies to bowel training. Through training, mishaps, and successes, the baby learns to control his anal muscles and to use the toilet. The fact that these muscles can be controlled should have suggested to us scientists that we should have been more cautious in describing the characteristics of the *"involuntary* nervous system."

In the area of sports, feedback has been used extensively for some years. During my days as a high school and college athlete, I became aware not only of the physical pleasure all athletes derive from learning what the body can do, but also of the dramatic effect of visual feedback. I watched how other athletes performed, and starting with junior high school, our football games were filmed. (It was not until college that I got to see basketball films of myself.)

Every Monday the team would troop in for the grading of the film of the past Saturday's game. We would be individually rated by each coach on each play. The head coach would then review the plays, sometimes showing one play a dozen times to point up a good or bad action. From this I could recognize the mistakes and visualize the best tackle, run, or pass. Of course, I loved the part of the film where I scored the winning touchdown, but the coach ran that play only twice. Although these "gradings" were an anxious time for us, they were an impressive learning experience. We learned from each other—our mistakes, our foolishness in appearance, and the exciting, beautiful plays that worked. I definitely became a more competent player because of this repeated visual feedback.

When playing basketball for Harvard, I was again fortunate to have this visual feedback. With the aid of basketball game films I came to realize how quick Bill Bradley, the famous Princeton basketball player, was. He was so smooth, we didn't realize his speed until we viewed the film in slow motion. One film in particular showed me how I could get my jump shot off more quickly. After copying some of Bradley's moves, I was able to replace him as the league-leading scorer the next year (luckily for me he had graduated).

Now we are exposed repeatedly to instant replays on TV. This has helped improve athletes' performances in all sports, but especially in football, basketball, golf, and tennis. All across the country youngsters are seeing and imitating Julius Irving in basketball, Bjorn Borg and Jimmy Connors in tennis, Johnny Miller in golf, and O. J. Simpson in football. By seeing these replays, they can begin practicing these moves by themselves and eventually use them in actual play.

One of the drawbacks of all this visual exposure is that young people see only their favorite athletes in the actual competitive event and in glamorous ads. All the training, pain, and disappointment go on behind the scenes.

What makes biofeedback different from these other forms of body feedback is its use of machines to help treat psychosomatic and stress-related disease. With the help of sophisticated machinery we are now able to control certain functions of our body previously thought to be beyond voluntary control. The machines serve a twofold purpose: (1) they give reliable, measurable information (making patients more aware of how their bodies function); and (2) they show patients the effects of their behavior on their bodies. By seeing that they can change what's happening, patients are encouraged to play an active role in their own well-being.

There are six principal diseases or disorders that have responded successfully to biofeedback training. They are tension headaches, primary Raynaud's disease, migraine headaches, muscular rehabilitation (spastic torticollis, stroke effects, fecal incontinence, etc.), labile and essential hypertension, and bruxism.

Biofeedback training is also quite useful for alleviating the pain and shortening the time of childbirth, certain types of insomnia, and chronic anxiety. Use of biofeedback for alleviation of other disorders such as menstrual pain, asthma, pain, cardiac arrhythmias, sexual disorders, and colitis appears promising. For these, however, I would suggest that the treatment be done by a trained doctor or psychiatrist or a clinical psychologist under the supervision of a doctor.

The treatment of the above disorders requires three conditions for positive clinical results: properly trained therapists, well-developed technology, and motivated patients.

Tension headaches are a prime example of a stress-related disease. These headaches are often described as feeling as if a vise is tightly bound around the head, particularly the forehead, with steady pain. The headaches are not thought to be caused by any organic or chemical condition, but by protracted contraction of face, scalp, and neck muscles.* The traditional treatment is reassurance, massage, aspirin, and phenobarbitol.

Tom Budzynski, Ph.D., Johann Stoyva, Ph.D., and Charles Adler, M.D., studied this problem and began treatment using the electromyograph (EMG) which measures muscle tension.† They found that by using EMG feedback, 79 percent of their patients showed significant declines in headaches.‡ They followed their control group and the treated patients for eighteen months to see if their control continued and their headaches decreased. Testing after four months and then eighteen months revealed that the patients continued to have significantly fewer tension headaches.

Using the methods of these researchers, it took four to eight weeks of two sessions per week to train patients to self-regulate these tension headaches. Work done by Drs. Bernard Gluck and Charles Stroebel (of the Hartford Institute of Living), myself, and many others supports the usefulness of this procedure. The treatment may take fourteen to

---

*L. Birk, "Biofeedback," *Behavioral Medicine*. New York, Grune & Stratton, 1973, p. 35.
† Ibid.
‡ Ibid.

twenty sessions, although some patients achieve relief in only eight to twelve sessions. It is exhilarating
for both the doctor and the patients to see these
patients go for two to three days and then a week
and more without a headache.

The following example will show how tension
headaches are treated through biofeedback.

Mr. M. was a 51-year-old professional actor who
had a 25-year history of tension headaches. He had
been in psychotherapy for approximately two years.
The initiation of an extramarital affair caused his
headaches to increase from two or three per month
to two to four per week. His headaches began to
have a serious effect on his career, and he began to
lose parts.

His therapist referred him to me for biofeedback
treatment. He was begun on EMG training and was
given specific physical and mental exercises to do
daily. After fourteen sessions he had not only
dropped his frontalis (forehead muscles) readings
from 28 to 3– 4 microvolts, but was able to maintain
these levels. As he had gone two weeks without a
headache, we stopped treatment. This patient also
reported two common side effects of this treatment:
falling asleep faster and less anxiety during stressful
situations. Whereas previously he had "hyped"
himself up in the typical "method" acting style before a performance, he now relaxed with biofeedback
exercises and felt more energy and freshness before
his actual performance. Thrilled with his success,
he referred for treatment another actor who had
been experiencing a great deal of anxiety before performances, and a woman whom he described as

tense and nervous. They also responded positively to this treatment.

My one-year follow-up on Mr. M. revealed that he had had only two slight headaches over the past year. In addition he had continued in psychotherapy after my treatment in order to work on his obsessive problems.

For the 20 to 30 percent of patients who do not respond to biofeedback training for tension headaches, I have prescribed other therapies. Many headache patients who were thought to be biofeedback failures were discovered to be depressives who did not need headache medication or tranquilizers but antidepressants and different forms of psychotherapy.

Raynaud's disease is another stress-related ailment. It is a circulatory problem that affects women five times more frequently than men. When under stress and/or when the external temperature is below 57 degrees, the hands blanch (turn white, blue, then red) and become quite painful. Patients often have a very cold hand temperature of 70 to 79 degrees, rather than the more normal temperature of 80 to 90 degrees. Previously the only treatments were for the patients (1) to go to a warm climate in the winter, (2) to have drugs injected to arrest the progression of the disease or (3) to have major surgery. In 0.5 percent of Raynaud's cases, this disease can lead to amputation.

Dr. Charles Stroebel recently developed a biofeedback treatment utilizing the electromyograph and peripheral skin temperature training that relieves the painful symptoms of Raynaud's disease in

90 percent of the cases. By 1976 he had already treated fifty patients successfully. I have been able to replicate his results using the same procedure. Earlier investigators have also reported success with single cases, and improvement was noted in four of the five cases.*

One case of Raynaud's disease was that of a 52-year-old professional woman, Ms. Y., who had suffered from the disease for over twenty years. Her physician was not in favor of drug treatment, and she tried to relieve the discomfort by wearing warm gloves, heavy socks, and boots. She still suffered during cold weather and achieved relief only when she went on vacation to Florida or Hawaii. She would be without symptoms as long as it was warm.

Upon hearing about the biofeedback work at the Hartford Institute of Living, she called them, and they referred her to me. She expressed some disbelief in her ability to learn to regulate these stress-related symptoms, but she was cooperative and agreed to do the home exercises. Her initial hand temperature was 71 degrees. After three basic relaxation sessions with EMG feedback, we began the actual peripheral skin temperature training (PSTT) with a thermister (registers finger temperature) taped to her fingers. After three or four sessions she began to achieve peripheral temperature increases of 1 or 2 degrees. In the last five sessions she was able to increase the temperature to 91 degrees. She had learned to increase her hand temperature 5 degrees within five minutes and to maintain a finger temperature above 90 degrees for fifteen minutes.

---

*Ibid, p. 121.

Her mental image for relaxing was a curtain descending slowly, as if night were falling. With this image she was able to bring the EMG reading of her forehead muscles down from 18 to 4 microvolts. Then, for warming her hands and feet, she used a mental image of herself lying in the sun on a beautiful beach. This helped her to learn to open (vasodilate) the arteries of her fingers and warm them above 90 degrees.

This patient has continued to be symptom-free after her one-year follow-up. She did not require further therapy. For other Raynaud's patients I have prescribed regular psychotherapy, psychoanalysis, group therapy, and dance therapy. These other therapies encourage the patients to continue to make the changes that are necessary to maintain their newly developed health. Without further therapy some of these patients might suffer a relapse or would not deal with the other stresses in their life.

Given the proper conditions mentioned before —an expert with a definite procedure, good technology, and a motivated patient—this disease can now be routinely alleviated.

Migraine headaches were discussed briefly earlier. Let's now look at a specific case.

Ms. G., a 32-year-old homemaker with two children, had suffered from migraine attacks for more than ten years. Even though her headaches were not totally incapacitating, they were quite painful. Approximately one-half hour before an attack, she would have warning signs that consisted of scintillating scotoma (a visual defect) and a vague feeling of sadness. Before coming to me, her migraine headaches were well controlled by her medication, which she took when she had these early warning signs.

The clinical biofeedback technique for the treatment of migraine is to train the person to warm her or his hands by vasodilation. Through this training the ability to vasodilate is then generalized so that there is less tendency for the arteries in the head to contract or go into spasm.

After three sessions of EMG training, Ms. G. began the peripheral skin temperature training (PSTT). After five sessions she was voluntarily able to warm her hands. Her migraine headaches dropped from one to two per week to none for the last two weeks of her training. The final two sessions were used to tune her control finely and to have her warm her hands without the biofeedback signals. She also received two sessions of other stress management techniques and suggestions about scheduling her time more effectively. At the one-year follow-up, she reported having had only one migraine attack, this occurring when her oldest child was seriously ill. She reported that she knows she controls the migraine because she can cause the scotoma to fade away.

With a good therapist and good training methods, 70 to 80 percent of migraine patients improve. Approximately 40 to 50 percent attain this improvement during the therapy period as described above. The other 30 to 40 percent require another two to three months of the specific exercises (mental and physical) to achieve voluntary control. Most of these do not need further treatment or therapy in the office, but need more time to establish control over the vascular spasm that causes the headache. They can be seen for a follow-up visit three months and again six months after treatment.

A word of caution: migraine and other headache patients must be examined by a physician and treated under his or her supervision because there might be other medical causes, such as possibly lethal tumors, for the headaches.

The *muscular rehabilitation* field has grown tremendously in the last two years. Here the object is to retrain muscles and muscle groups that have been damaged through disease or accidents. If stroke victims have lost certain muscle functions because of damage, they can slowly be retrained to contract more and more muscle groups. The EMG gives them feedback even if the limbs don't move. In each session they hear, see, and soon feel the muscles contracting via the feedback information, usually in the form of clicks, lights, or a dial display. They rarely become discouraged if the finger or hand does not always move, because they can see their work pay off—they have evidence that the muscles are alive and working. Dr. Joseph Brudny of New York University Medical Center has established a sensory feedback therapy unit and accepts patients suffering from strokes, spastic torticollis, and dystonic forms of cerebral palsy. His results have created new treatments for these distressing conditions.

Worthwhile programs are going on in muscle rehabilitation centers across the United States. For information call your local hospital or medical society, or write to the Biofeedback Research Society, University of Colorado Medical Center,

4200 East Ninth Avenue, Denver, Colorado 80220.

One of the more exquisite studies of muscle retraining was done by Drs. Bernard Engel and M. Schuster. They were able to restore bowel control in six out of seven patients by retraining the patients to control the external and internal sphincter. (They have now successfully treated over thirty patients.) These patients had suffered loss of bowel control because of general neurological disorders, direct injury to the anal sphincter, or spinal injuries. They learned or relearned to control their bowel movements in three or four, two-hour sessions. After a period of one to five years they still retained control. Dr. Schuster, the psychiatrist and gastroenterologist, stated, "In our experience and that of others using the technique, learning is gratifyingly rapid. Patients can learn almost as if by insight."[*] He further pointed out that once having learned control, patients maintained it without further treatment or reinforcement.

Hypertension is one of the most difficult psychosomatic diseases to work with since practically any stressor will cause changes in the blood pressure. Even in the face of this difficulty, success ratios of from 50 to 60 percent have been reported by Dr. Chandra Patel[†] and myself.[‡] Drs. David Shapiro, Gary Schwartz, Bernard Tursky; Neal Miller and his co-workers; and Charles Stroebel as well as

---

[*]M. Schuster, "Operant Conditioning," *Hospital Practice,* September 1974, p. 143.
[†]C. Patel, "Twelve Months' Following of Yoga and Biofeedback in the Management of Hypertension," *Lancet,* January 11, 1975, pp. 62-65.
[‡]The information on my work on hypertension and treatment of Raynaud's disease was presented in February 1976 at the Annual Biofeedback Research Society meetings at Colorado Springs, Colorado.

others have also reported success in training patients to decrease their blood pressure.

Dr. Patel has treated over 60 patients and I have treated over 25. I want to summarize this work for you. In Dr. Patel's first report on 20 patients she found that 5 patients (25 percent) were able to learn to reduce their blood pressure (BP) and stop their medication entirely. Seven others (35 percent) learned to decrease their BP and reduced their medication by 35 percent to 60 percent. BP control was better in 4 others (20 percent) and the other 4 patients showed no change in BP.

In her most recent study (FN page 108) with a treatment group and a control group there were similar results with BP decreases from an average of 168/100 to 141/84—an average of approximately 27 points systolic and 16 points diastolic. Furthermore, when she treated the control group, they showed similar decreases in BP, and no members of the treated group showed an increase in BP.*

My work in treating hypertensives with similar techniques showed an average decrease in the two treatment groups of 26.5 systolic and 12.8 diastolic for the first group (treated with EMG and PSTT) and 16.1 systolic and 10.8 diastolic in the second (treated with EMG and GSR).

Treatment consists of using PSTT, EMG, and GSR (galvanic skin response that measures skin perspiration) therapy with physical exercises and mental imagery. Although the treatment of hypertension through biofeedback is relatively new, these results have been most encouraging.

---

*C. Patel, "Yoga and Biofeedback in the Management of Hypertension," *The Lancet,* November 10, 1973, p. 1053.

In *bruxism,* a disorder in which the jaw muscles are overly tense and the teeth are being ground down, the EMG is used to train for less muscle tension or contraction. The patient gains control over these muscles in much the same way as the tension headache patient learns vasodilation.

While citing the "success" statistics of biofeedback, we would do well to keep in mind the subtle effects of the emotions in the cause and treatment of disease. It is generally agreed that up to 30 percent of the "improved" patients in any given survey may be simply responding to their own expectation of improvement from treatment, not to any specific learned action. This placebo effect must be taken into consideration in any study. To have a clinically effective treatment, doctors try to achieve a 50 to 60 percent success range. If a study shows only 30 percent success or improvement, there may be other factors, such as patient selection (picking sicker or better patients) or "new treatment," that could explain the apparent improvement. Thus you should be suspicious of spontaneous cures or of so-called cures that occur in only 30 percent of patients involved in a new treatment program.

Dr. Stroebel has suggested that we use this placebo effect to the patients' advantage by capitalizing on their belief in the treatment to show them how they can become responsible for their own health. He states:

Modern medicine probably does not sufficiently emphasize this need for individual responsibility. Acclimated as he is to being a recipient rather than a participant in treatment, modern man may require personal demonstration through a structured period of self learning to incorporate the concept of individual responsibility into his daily lifestyle in times of both health and illness. Biofeedback may serve as an optimal procedure for a structured self learning experience, since the individual can learn firsthand about regulating the effects of daily stress on body functioning.*

The final group we must look at are those who appear not to respond to biofeedback—the "failures." Again we suspect that emotional rather than physical factors are at work. For example, in the treatment of Raynaud's disease, the failure rate seems to be 5 to 10 percent, whereas in migraine headaches the rate is 20 to 30 percent. Since both treatments require the learning of similar physiological skills by patients, which they have the ability to master, we must ask why the failure rate of headache patients is so much higher?

There are two probable causes. One is that some people are restless, paranoid, and often unwilling to attend therapy sessions and to do the exercises, either in treatment or on their own. Fortunately, there are very few patients like this, and their unwillingness is frequently a sign of serious personality difficulties.

A far larger group, however, are people who are depressed or who receive a secondary gain from their illness, meaning that some other rewards or supports are present (consciously or unconsciously) that maintain the symptom or disease. Thus, if the tension or migraine headaches are presenting subtle or not so subtle rewards (e.g., you don't have to do

*L. Birk, "Biofeedback," *Behavioral Medicine.* New York, Grune & Stratton, 1973, p. 32.

your job because of your illness, or you are given greater sympathy and support because of your pain), the patient unconsciously *may not be able or willing to give up these symptoms.* In fact, if during biofeedback training the symptoms start to disappear, these patients may become depressed, sicker, or suicidal. They tend to stop treatment or come late, be restless, not follow directions, and practice at home sporadically, if at all.

In these cases longer and different therapies are required and should be undertaken with a psychiatrist or psychotherapist who is trained to deal with these severe symptoms. For those who are clearly psychotic, biofeedback appears to be of little or no help at all. Biofeedback requires the patients' cooperation. Therefore, before it can work, the patients must at least be capable of working for their own well-being.

8.
How Biofeedback Saved the Life of a Friend

Matthew J. Culligan

The contemplated suicide of a very good friend of mine impelled me toward biofeedback. My friend was the losing candidate for the presidency of one of the Fortune 500 (the 500 largest corporations in the world). By general consensus, he was the better man for the job, but the scale was tipped toward his opponent by the people who controlled the company through family stock ownership.

The contest lasted two years, with subtle but brutal pressures accumulating as the battle neared its climax. My friend's migraine and tension headaches started along the way. Typically, they increased in severity and frequency as the pressure mounted. Eventually, they became so agonizing that his physician recommended shots that literally put him out for hours. He feared travel, and he made only those trips that were unavoidable. In these cases, his doctor equipped him with a traveling kit to enable him to give himself shots when the headache became unbearable.

My concern for him mounted and peaked at a Caribbean resort where we had gone to play golf with business colleagues. When I stopped at his room to tell him our transportation was waiting, he came to the door looking dreadfully distraught and ill. He had been unable to sleep, and because of his obligation to play golf, he had not been taking his shots. It was then that he said, his eyes half-crazed, "I can't go on."

I did what I could, which was damned little. He accepted my urging to forget the golf, take his shot, and get home as soon as possible.

Fate had already taken a hand in this grim affair. Earlier that same month I had met an extraordinary young man who was involved in a new treatment. He spoke knowingly, glowingly, almost passionately about a new technique and technology called biofeedback. I didn't appreciate the name because it had the promotional ring of the buzz word. Besides, for three decades I had witnessed, even been a part of, a long parade of revolutionary concepts calculated, at the very least, to change the world.

But something about this young man did command my attention and respect. That, plus the pressing need of my suicidal friend, cemented my interest in investigating biofeedback self-regulation training.

What I learned from this young man was quite promising, and his credibility grew as I probed him for his personal and professional background. He checked out positively on all surface characteristics. I was particularly impressed by his apparent dedication and by the sacrifices he had made to be a frontrunner in biofeedback.

My interest redoubled when he described his involvement with Dr. Elmer Green, of the famed Menninger Clinic. He had avidly devoured all the written output of Dr. Green, one of the prophets and guiding spirits of biofeedback. Then he visited the clinic and spent hours with Dr. Green and his daughter, who works as Dr. Green's associate. He came back totally committed to biofeedback, not as just another concept, but as the synthesis of many concepts that had varying degrees of acceptance and longevity.

The Menninger connection and the possibility that biofeedback could survive as a kind of model for all attempts at self-control finally convinced me to make two decisions: first, to get my troubled friend to see my new acquaintance, or to go to Menninger if necessary; second, to give management and financial support to this new field.

The effect of biofeedback training on my friend was magical, though complicated. So exhausted was he from the sleepless nights and debilitating attacks that instead of going into and remaining in a relaxed state in which the biofeedback self-regulation training could be done, my friend would go into a deep sleep for hours. My young friend was forced to tiptoe quietly out of the room when his patient went to sleep, telling my friend's wife to notify him when he awoke.

To this day I don't know to what degree the hours of *sleep* contributed to the gradual improvement of my friend, but the experiment worked. The drops into sleep became less frequent, and the actual biofeedback training commenced. The severity of the headaches decreased, as did the frequency. At the end of three months, my friend had his first full week without a headache. We celebrated and both had a *hangover* headache, which became a cause of glee. Then my friend got cocky, missed some sessions, failed to do his homework with a galvanic skin response unit, and came back one day very contrite, having had his first attack in two months. He has been a model of steadfastness ever since.

On the basis of this and what I was learning about biofeedback, I organized financial support for and co-founded, a company called Q-tran, Ltd., a word play on tranquility, the hope for us all.

A location was found, painted, decorated, and furnished in a kind of funky way, that led a lady of conservative taste to describe the place "as what I've always thought a whorehouse would look like."

The decor was camp, the occupants ranged from mod to bizarre. It looked like a hippie hangout in Greenwich Village. Long-haired people of all ages —tieless, shirtless, shoeless, deodorantless, brain-less—flocked to Q-tran, consumed oceans of coconut and papaya juice, sprawled on every tabletop and other piece of furniture, and damn near ruined the noble experiment in its first two months. I was close to despair, contemplating the loss of about $50,000, and the embarrassment of facing friends and associates to whom I had introduced biofeedback with such hope.

But something was happening below the chaotic surface. Doctors, dentists, psychiatrists, psychologists, and therapists came out of curiosity but also with suspicion. Science writers also came, ready to find the flaws. After meeting with the staff and getting a demonstration of the machines, many went away reluctantly conceding that we might be able to do some good. Doctors referred patients, to whom they could prescribe only drugs and panaceas, and improvements were noted. Q-tran survived, but a new name seemed appropriate; we christened it the Stress Transformation Center.

Through the months of September, October, and November 1973, the Stress Transformation Center averaged around twenty clients, or trainees (we dared not call them patients) a month and achieved some heartwarming results.

In this highly constructive phase a critical new element entered the control equation; it was called, appropriately, the onset cue. My abhorrence for cute, quasi-scientific jargon didn't apply here because onset and cue were understandable words individually and together. As I developed my own understanding of emotion, thinking, communication, and control, I saw how the onset cue fit into the mosaic as the early warning system. Onset cues were inadvertently suggested through treatment of a beautiful lady I fell in love with. I was quite smitten until I gradually realized that she smoked like a Con Ed tower, drank like Brendan Behan, and kept the hours of a night owl. We rapidly became platonic friends, she because of boredom at 3 a.m. and I because of exhaustion.

When the passion left, understanding arrived. My ex-love told me she had suffered from migraines since her late teens. The pain was excruciating, and she needed large quantities of pills or an injection to keep her from banging her head against the wall.

She agreed to meet me at the clinic and to then make up her mind about a course of training. The first meeting was a disaster; one of the staff associates gave a credible lecture titled "Energy Maximization by Biofeedback Technique" and then, before my horrified eyes, *fell asleep*. My ex-love's withering look needed no supplementary words. I used reverse psychology with her, asking "Do you think

I'd be involved with this and those nuts if there weren't something below the surface?" She looked thoughtful and said, "I suppose not."

She did agree, finally, to a course of ten 90-minute sessions, and made slow, steady progress. The principal problem was that nothing we recommended helped after she had started a migraine. But she reported fewer attacks as a result of the training session. That is when I first heard about onset cues.

She was queried exhaustively about what happened *before* the attacks—what she felt, thought, observed. I gave the first clue. She had merry, lively blue eyes, that I loved to look into. I noticed on a few occasions that her left eye seemed to "look funny," as though it were out of focus. I mentioned this fact to the staff head; he almost shouted "Eureka!" remembering a migraine episode at the Menninger Clinic in which the patient's eyes were affected as the blood engorgement intensified. Our client was told to carry a hand mirror at all times and to look at herself periodically. She did so, and called in great excitement on a Monday, after a weekend away, with the news that her left eye seemed "cloudy and out of focus" about ten minutes before the onset of a migraine—this was her onset cue. Her progress after that discovery was rapid. Whenever her left eye started to cloud, she would do her prescribed relaxation exercises and short-circuit the headache before it got to the painful stage.

Discovering the onset cue was made an integral part of the training. But the most obvious cue was cold hands. Normal hand temperature is between 80 and 90 degrees, and temperatures below this mark indicate tension or distress. If the temperature of the hands is below 80 degrees, they are cold. If it is below 75 degrees, they are very cold. Several businessmen who came to our center suffering from migraine or stress-related headaches were instructed to put their hands to their cheek during stressful situations. If the hands felt cold, they were told to get up, make some excuse, and temporarily absent themselves from the situation. They were given a brief biofeedback exercise that could be done almost anywhere to warm their hands and relax their body.

I have had considerable personal experience with this practice of warming parts of the body. Some years ago, as mentioned earlier, I had corrective surgery done on my left leg to improve the blood flow and to prevent circulation problems that would crop up as I got older. A few hours after coming out of the anesthetic, I started doing my biofeedback routine of mental relaxation and began directing my blood to my left leg—no difficult feat after two years' practice. The doctor dropped by to tell me that the operation had gone routinely and that he would visit me the next morning.

The next morning, a half-hour before he was due, I arranged myself as comfortably as possible, meditated, and then directed blood to my left leg. I knew I was getting results as the sole of my left foot became warm and tingly.

The doctor was punctual. From the doorway, he asked, "How are you?" As I said "Fine," he came to the foot of the bed, reached out, took hold of my five toes, and smiled appreciatively, saying, "Oh, very very good." I asked him to feel my right foot. He did, and his eyebrows rose expressively and quizzically. "It's cooler," he said. I held out my hands; he held them. "They're cooler too," he said.

I then told him of my biofeedback exercises. He nodded his head, and said, "Very interesting," without skepticism. He was thoughtful as he left, saying, "Whatever it is, it works—keep it up."

My rate of healing was rapid, very rapid, I think. I walked over a mile six days later, two miles eight days after the operation and, with the help of a walking stick, played eighteen holes of golf eleven days after. This is put forward not as scientific research or as a promise of any kind, but simply as a personal experience that is not uncommon for those who have worked at some form of body control.

Another contribution I was able to make to the clinic was the introduction of the word "tessitura." This is a term that describes the general range of vocal highs and lows.

I had noticed a decade earlier that my voice seemed to change when I was under great pressure. Enlisting the aid of my favorite sound engineer from the weekend radio show *Monitor*, I had my voice recorded when I felt totally relaxed. The engineer then installed a recorder in my office which I could activate by pushing a lever. During several very tense episodes involving office politics, when my voice would seem to me to be changing, I would unobtrusively turn on the recorder and tape a few minutes of my speech.

We put both voice tracks on twin oscilloscopes, and compared the normal and stressed tracks. The difference was instantly obvious. Here was my onset cue. I had a floor button installed that alerted my secretary. When I touched it once, she would announce a very important incoming call. If it rang twice, she would poke her head in and ask me to step out to sign a contract. The moment I detected any variation in my voice, I would (having given my secretary the appropriate signal) get on the telephone, nod, saying, "Yes, yes," "That's good," or some such remark, and try to relax. If more than that was necessary, I would leave the office for a minute or so and do some stretching or bending exercises and deep rhythmic breathing. In this way I alleviated my distress. In retrospect, I am convinced that my present remarkably good health is due in part to recognition of my onset cue.

My enthusiasm over onset cues lasted until I discussed them with Dr. Sedlacek. His reaction was one of tolerant amusement. He made the point that I was dealing with the *superficial* aspects of stress which, he said, was all well and good, but his interest was in the steps *before* the onset cues appeared. There were identifiable, medical reasons for onset cues. What were they? What could be done at an earlier, preventive level?

Episodes such as this confirmed the wisdom of writing this book with a person who was a psychiatrist, in addition to being young and open-minded enough to study biofeedback as part of the whole problem of stress. Dr. Sedlacek did not discourage experimentation and argument, but he drew the line on exposition of unproved theories or superficial research to a public craving for new answers, new solutions to vexing problems.

As the number of reputable professionals with impeccable credentials have proven their results and published them in medical journals, the opposition to biofeedback has begun to fade. Increasingly those within the medical profession have begun to see that biofeedback treatment under proper circumstances has a great deal to offer in helping to alleviate stress-related disease.

The only substantive question remaining is that of the future of biofeedback. Will it slip out of primary focus and be just another passing fad, to be replaced by yet another "hot" concept? We trust not, because biofeedback is a living, changing concept under whose philosophical umbrella all other concepts can be amiably accommodated.

In a curious way biofeedback is a little cog in the great wheel described by Arnold Toynbee as the hope of the human race for survival. He wrote that the human race had a chance of survival through the interpenetration of the East and the West—the Western world if it could slow down its self-destructive race for more machines and armaments and learn from the contemplative and meditative teachings of the ancient East; the Eastern world if it could accept the technologies and techniques of the West for the solution of its eons-old problems of poverty, misery, ignorance, and disease. Biofeedback happily accepted and employed many of the lessons and teachings of the ancient religions on breathing, diet, contemplation, and meditation. It simultaneously accommodated some of the useful developments of the behavior scientists, who caused an information blizzard on behavior modification. The acceptance of biofeedback technology was the easiest to achieve, because doctors and scientists are conditioned from school days to the use of diagnostic machinery.

The next chapter is devoted to the description of biofeedback technology. A wide range of electronic and electric equipment has been devised (not invented, since all components have existed for years) to aid doctors in biofeedback research and training.

We urge you to see beyond the technology sweeping the biofeedback field. It is the human body, mind, and emotions that are paramount. What we seek is thought, communication, and control to reach the ultimate goals of greater health and happiness.

9.
Biofeedback Machinery and What to Look For in Selecting a Clinic or Doctor

Keith Sedlacek, M.D.

A brief history of biofeedback will be helpful before we consider the technology since most of the machinery was designed first for laboratory research and was modified or adapted for specific research work and then for clinical work.

The "grandfather" of biofeedback is Neal Miller of Rockefeller University. The work he did in the fifties and early sixties in conflict behavior, motivation, and social learning set the stage for biofeedback research. His article in *Science,* "Learning of Visceral and Glandular Response," in 1969, opened the path for research into the self-regulation of the functions of the autonomic system in both rats and man.

Through his work, a number of formerly held beliefs were changed. He showed that the autonomic system (the internal machinery of our body), which controls visceral response, previously thought to be beyond man's control, could be trained and reinforced by rewards. This visceral learning was specific; that is, rats and humans can change their heartrate without influencing other autonomic controlled variables, such as breathing rates, and blood pressure, and vice versa.

Miller stated:

Biofeedback should be well worth trying on any symptom, functional or organic, that is under neural control, that can be continuously monitored by modern instrumentation, and for which a given direction of change is clearly indicated medically ... for example, cardiac arrhythmias, spastic colitis, and asthma, and those cases of high blood pressure that are not essential compensation for kidney damage.*

I recommend this article to all of you who are reading this book.

In 1971, exceptional publicity was given to the work of Joe Kamiya with the electroencephalograph (EEG)—and the hoopla over alpha waves began. The press played up the fact that through training we could learn to regulate or influence our brain waves and touted it as a great discovery, but I think Dr. Miller has more accurately described the current results of alpha training:

Many subjects report that high levels of alpha are associated with a relaxing, pleasant experience; and some give glowing testimonials of effects of alpha training, ranging from relief of tension to greatly increased creativity. But a few subjects report undesirable feelings, such as being out of control, while alpha predominated in their EEG. Considerable use is being made of alpha feedback by both trained and untrained therapists, and energetic entrepreneurs are selling their devices for take-home, do-it-yourself training; but in striking contrast with such enthusiasm, to date there seems to be virtually no evidence, well controlled for placebo effects, of any specific therapeutic value from such training.†

---

*N. Miller, "Learning of Visceral and Glandular Response," *Science,* vol. 163, 1969, p. 434.
†N. Miller, Kaplan et al., eds., in *Comprehensive Textbook of Psychiatry.* Baltimore, Williams & Wilkins, 1974, p. 358.

The publicity about alpha waves, however, spawned the production of a flood of commercially available EEG units. Exaggerated claims were made by the largely untrained people who were using these machines, and many people were "treated" (at varying fees) with little or no success. Biofeedback, which the public associated with alpha waves, began to get a bad name. (The situation has become so bad that some researchers have told me that they cannot be funded if they mention biofeedback in their grant proposals. Many doctors have taken to separating themselves from the alpha phenomenon by using such names as "sensory feedback" in their work.) Serious research *is* being done in the brain-wave field, but as yet there are no clinical treatments that have been demonstrated and published.

A major breakthrough occurred in 1972, when Drs. Elmer Green and Joseph Sargent, from the Menninger Foundation, published their work on migraine headaches.* This placed the temperature unit alongside the EEG, EMG, and GSR as the main research and treatment units in biofeedback. These training units were handmade for Green and Sargent by engineers at Menninger.

In 1973 Drs. Tom Budzynski and Johann Stoyva published their work on tension headache,† which provided solid and controlled data supporting EMG treatment of tension headache.

Drs. Charles Stroebel and Joseph Brudny furthered the clinical base for treatment of migraine

---

*J. Sargent, E. Green, and E. Walters, "The Use of Autogenic Feedback Training in a Pilot Study of Migraine and Tension Headache," *Headache,* vol. 12, 1972, p. 120.
†In L. Birk, p. 35.

headache, tension headache, Raynaud's disease, and muscular rehabilitation in 1974 when they began to present their findings.

These investigations, along with many others, such as those done by John V. Basmajian, M.D., and Barbara Brown, Ph.D., have now created an enlarging field for research and clinical application. As more applications have become apparent, there has been a burgeoning of equipment manufacturers.

Let me briefly describe the major biofeedback machines. The therapeutic use of the galvanic skin response (GSR) dates back to Jung's use of it, in 1906 and 1907, in his association test. The GSR measures autonomic arousal by recording the changing resistance of the skin. The major component here is the sympathetically controlled sweat gland. The more the subject perspires, the more the machine reacts. The biofeedback GSR, instead of recording this information on a piece of paper, feeds the information back to the therapist and patient by sound or sight. Thus, by reducing the sympathetic arousal, the sound would decrease in pitch. The GSR is one component of the lie detector. It records the sympathetic response that usually is associated with lying. In training with this unit, the patient can explore both high and low levels of sympathetic arousal. This machine also has an application in psychotherapy as an identifier of emotionally charged material. (As the patient deals with matters that are important to him, his skin moisture increases, and the GSR picks up even the slightest change in the amount of this moisture.)

The electromyograph has also been in clinical use for years and has been used to measure and record muscle contraction and nerve conductance. By completing the feedback loop with a signal to the patient, we create a learning situation. Thus we can train for less and less muscle contraction, as in treating tension headaches, or for more and more contraction, for better control and a fuller range of movement in muscle rehabilitation. By using EMG training, an individual can experience states of muscle relaxation far deeper than are experienced by others in their everyday life.

There has been a tendency to do more work with the EMG (and consequently more sophisticated units of it have been developed) because so far it has yielded the best clinical results for tension headaches, spastic torticollis, and muscular rehabilitation. This is so partly because this instrument is the most easily demonstrated to a patient. That is, patients can more easily accept the relationship between tightening their muscles and seeing the dial swing right or left or hearing more clicks, reflecting more tension. Then they relax a muscle, say, of the forearm, and see the dial swing back and the clicks slow down. Since patients have had this experience before, of tightening and relaxing the muscle, the EMG unit "fits" their belief system more easily. This is less so in the case of the temperature and EEG units. With these machines, patients have to develop a relationship to the machine. Their ability to believe in their own power to influence their physiology seems to play a large part in the development, or lack of it, of better physiological self-regulation.

The temperature unit is a sensitive thermister (usually attached to the fingers or hands) that is generally calibrated to show changes of 0.1 to 0.2 degrees. Again the feedback loop is closed by giving the information of the moment-to-moment temperature change back to the patient via a signal. Dr. Green developed these units as a clinical device in his treatment of patients with migraine headaches.

The electroencephalograph (EEG) has also been a research and clinical tool for years. Brain tumors, epilepsy, and other clinical diseases have been diagnosed from tracings of the electrical output of the brain. However, it wasn't until Tom Mulholland, Ph.D., and later Joe Kamiya, fed back this information that we realized that we could influence this electrical output of the brain.

There are four main brain waves: beta, alpha, theta, and delta. In the usual waking state, the frequency most often picked up by the surface electrodes placed on the scalp is beta. Alpha waves are seen in approximately 90 percent of people when they close their eyes and relax. Alpha is also reported in meditation, with more alpha density being recorded by those more experienced in this practice. Theta waves are generally recorded when a person is drowsy or falling asleep. Delta waves are normally seen only when a person is sleeping.

It is interesting to note that the EEG and EMG were particularly helped by the miniaturization of components that developed out of the Space Program. This allowed for more sensitivity in smaller units, lessening the need for the bulky research models.

These are the basic units of biofeedback, although other ingenious instruments have proven to be useful in other research and treatment. For example, in Dr. Engel's work with incontinence, he used two specially devised "balloons" to record and feed back the muscle contraction of the anal sphincters.* Drs. David Shapiro and Gary Schwartz developed a machine that registered the blood pressure of human subjects and fed the information back to them. They showed that volunteers could influence their blood pressure.†

In short, almost any machine that records information about an event that is recognized by and can be made available to the patient for learning can be adapted for biofeedback. It is like the old game of hot-cold, in which a person locates an object as another responds to his movements with "hot" or "cold" as he moves closer to or farther away from the object. In biofeedback the machine and the therapist cue the patients as to whether they are "hot" or "cold," until the patients can feel and control the particular physiological variables themselves.

The biofeedback equipment available varies widely in quality. Manufacturers of standard medical equipment entered the field by adapting existing models initially for research and then for treatment. Their units cost from $3,000 to $10,000. Firms specializing in feedback equipment have grown out of their connection with biofeedback research. Some of these firms are Biofeedback Systems, Boulder, Colorado; Cyborg, Boston, Massachusetts; and Autogenics Systems, Inc., Berkeley, California. Their equipment is of good quality and generally costs

---

*B. Engel and M. Schuster, "Operant Conditioning of Rectosphincteric Responses in the Treatment of Fecal Incontinence," *New England Journal of Medicine,* vol. 290, 1974, p. 646.
†In L. Birk, pp. 133-143.

from $600 to $3500 per unit. Smaller, take-home models of varying quality are also available for $50 to $400. I have used a home GSR made by the Biofeedback Instrument Company of New York with good results. Finally, there is, unfortunately, a great deal of worthless equipment on the market. Before you buy any equipment, check it out with a reputable clinic, medical society, or other objective source. Ethical biofeedback firms sell equipment only to professionals.

All biofeedback equipment should be checked for safety, reliability, and endurance. In particular, EEG units may have a wide difference of quality and capability. The government appears to be moving toward declaring this equipment to fall under the category of medical devices. Once this happens, it will begin to establish specific standards for manufacturers.

Once we are using accurate, up-to-date machinery, we must look to the therapist and the patients to discover whether the treatment will be effective. Perhaps the most important factor in successful biofeedback training is a qualified therapist who is not only technically skilled, but able to elicit the most cooperative response from the patients. The patients must be motivated as well as willing to learn to adopt an attitude of passive volition—a state in which they will something to happen but don't force it. It appears that this attitude of "passive volition" is necessary to allow physiological change to happen. For this reason, it is crucial that the therapist maintain an atmosphere as relaxing and pressure-free for the patient as possible.

To me, the clearest explanation of passive volition is Elmer Green's explanation and diagram, which he has allowed me to reproduce here:

"Biofeedback is both simple and persuasive. Perhaps the most surprising biofeedback demonstration for most people is learning to control their own hand temperature. . . .

"To 'learn' temperature control, a person both imagines and tries to 'feel' his hands getting warm. If he attempts to force it, the temperature usually drops, and we can say, 'That is lesson number 1; don't do it that way.' The trainee soon discovers that when the desired change is visualized and felt in a certain way, the body will comply as long as the accompanying emotional stance is detached, non-anxious, merely expectant. We call this physiological process 'passive volition,' in order to distinguish it from 'active volition,' the kind of 'will power' used to shovel snow, through control of normally voluntary physiological processes.

"Whether control of normally unconscious processes can eventually be exercised through active volition, after training, is an interesting theoretical question, but there is no longer any doubt that voluntary control of many involuntary processes can be learned with the aid of biofeedback.

"It is clear that there can be no theoretical objection to the idea that the neurological and biochemical balances that underlie healthy well-being (psychosomatic health) can be disturbed by psychological pressures, and behaviorally it is an observed fact. Psychological changes are converted by the biological machinery into neurological and hormonal responses. This is not news for those involved in limbic and hypothalamic research, but volition and its psychoneuro-hormonal correlates have not yet been brought into the picture in a scientific way. Volition has been an existential embarrassment to scientists for about three generations, and volition exercised through biofeedback is not intensifying the stress level because many of its effects take place in the observable 'involuntary' physiological domain.

FIGURE 5.

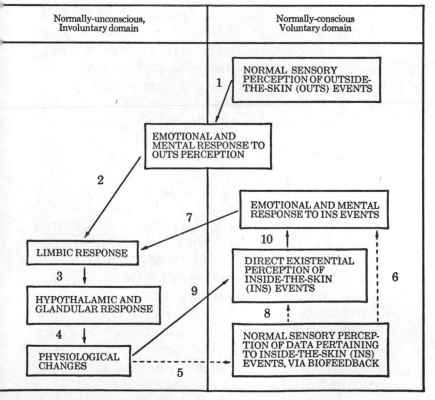

igure 5. Biocybernetic loop in which physiological reaction to outside-the-skin
OUTS) events can be modified by perception of inside-the-skin (INS) events, through
he use of biofeedback.

"Arrows 1 and 2 of Figure 1 (page 25) indicate the sensory-emotion-limbic pathways through which psychological stress, originating outside the skin (OUTS), triggers physiological responses. The biofeedback loop used in learning voluntary control of normally-unconscious processes includes arrows 3 through 7. During biofeedback training, while voluntary skill is being developed, arrow 8 gradually comes into existence. Later, when voluntary skill is fully developed, arrow 9 supplants arrows 5, 6, and 8; that is, direct existential perception of inside-the-skin (INS) processes develops. Biofeedback is then no longer necessary in order to know what is happening in the body and the biofeedback section can be dropped out of the cybernetic loop. The convergence of arrows 2 and 7 in the diagram indicates the combining of INS and OUTS data. In some indeterminate way, volition can modify the 'action' in arrows 6 and 10 and change the overall state of dynamic balance in the system. . . .

"Without defining volition, purposeful changes can be made in the psychophysiological-biofeedback system. Biofeedback provides an immediate indication of inside-the-skin (INS) behavior, just as the temperature detector in a thermostat provides immediate information for the thermal control system. Biofeedback makes it possible for a person to know when he is succeeding in his effort to modify an involuntary physiological process. The basic factor which is felt existentially and is defined only operationally is volition.

"Keeping the diagram of Figure 1(page 25) in mind and returning to the matter of active

and passive volition, the normally involun-
tarily, unconscious, sections of one's self can be
induced to behave in ways that are consciously
chosen by visualizing what is wanted, asking
the being (body, mind, brain, unconscious, or
whatever) to do it, and then detaching oneself
from the results. A symbolic way of putting it is
to say that the cortex plants the impulse in the
subcortex and then allows nature to take its
course without interference. This is passive volition.

"The operational process suggested in the
phrase 'the cortex plants' may find an analogy
in farming. There seems to be a correspondence
between human physiological responses to volition and the way 'nature' responds in general
to human initiative. For instance, a farmer (a)
desires a crop, (b) plants the seed, (c) allows nature to take its course, and (d) reaps. In a corre-
sponding way, a migraine patient first desires
and visualizes a certain kind of physiological
behavior. This is a conscious 'cortical' process.
Next he plants the idea in the unconscious, the
'earth' of one's psychological being. Now nature
is allowed to take its course. The patient pas-
sively allows his psychophysiological machinery to function, without anxiety or analytically
'picking at' what he is trying existentially to do.
The farmer does not dig up his seeds to see if
they are sprouting. He has 'faith' that they will
sprout and allows nature to implement the process he has initiated. Finally, the migraine
patient 'reaps' vascular stability, a completely
natural process.

"Psychosomatic disease can be thought of,
in the above context, as a distortion that begins

when psychological stress is allowed to disrupt the normal neurohumoral sequences of physiological events. For clarity, it is necessary to point out that 'stress' is used here in a technical sense. Stress, by definition, is the force applied to a structure. 'Strain' is the amount that the structure yields. Any mechanical structure (or physiological process) that is strained beyond its elastic limit cannot regain its original shape (or function) when the stress is relieved unless an outside force is applied in the opposite direction. In an analogous way, a temporary powerful psychological stress can strain the human physiological apparatus beyond its limits. Reference to this phenomenon is repeatedly heard in such phrases as 'she never looked the same again' or 'his hair turned white overnight.'

"From a theoretical point of view it is not necessary for a stress to be overpoweringly traumatic in order to result in psychosomatic disorder. For example, an insult is generally a momentary stress, but if the emotional strain is 'allowed' to persist by means of mnemonic reiteration (repetition of the stress symbol), appropriate physiological changes must necessarily take place. The homeostatic, elastic, restoring forces in biological processes differ from person to person, but a general psychosomatic hypothesis seems to be well supported, namely: A chronic emotional strain is accompanied by chronic changes in physiological homeostasis. Considerable neurological and biochemical evidence in support of the above concepts are scattered throughout the literature on psychosomatic disease.

"Self-regulation concepts were difficult to

apply until biofeedback came into the mind-body picture as a new and powerful tool. Biofeedback closes the biocybernetic (signals from the body back to the body) loop by developing awareness of INS (inside-the-skin) behavior."[*]

This is the control system each of us has working for us. If we get in better touch with the internal events of our bodies, we can better self-regulate our health.

With the awareness of the amazing control system we possess, more attention is being paid to extraordinary feats of body control that have occurred and are occurring. One remarkable story was reported by Dr. Green, who traveled to India to study some of the masters of the Eastern religions. He was put in contact with a man called Swami Rama, who claimed to "stop his heart." Upon demonstration, Green discovered that, actually, the Swami's heart went into fibrillation—that is, the heart muscle contracted in a random manner and blood was not pushed purposefully out of the heart. Usually fibrillation requires that an electric shock be applied by doctors to reintegrate the heart's proper pumping action. The Swami evidently had significant "control" over his heart muscle because he "restarted" his heart.

Dr. Green also discovered that the Swami could voluntarily cause a 2-degree temperature difference from one side of his hand to the other. Dr. Wes Lynch while working in Neal Miller's lab has dem-

---

[*]E. Green and A. Green, "Regulating Our Mind Processes." Paper delivered at 6th Annual Medical Meeting of the ARE CLINIC, Phoenix, January 1973.

onstrated that one subject could cause different temperatures in each of his hands.* Earlier in 1968, Miller had trained rats to produce vasodilation in one ear and either no change or vasoconstriction in the other.†

These cases of temperature control are becoming more common. Barbara Pearce, formerly a researcher at the Menninger Foundation, now at Loma Linda Medical Center, told me of a patient who was trapped in a snowslide with a group of people. One man had been trained to warm his hands and, realizing that he would be rescued in a few hours, proceeded to direct warmth to his hands. When the group was rescued, he was the only person who did not have frostbitten fingers.

Joe Culligan has already related how he was able to direct more blood to his injured leg to speed the healing process. The implications of these cases are vast. The advantages of body control are evident, and we have only begun to discover what we can do.

It would appear that biofeedback will continue to be a main source of new information about the body as long as the treatment and the machinery are of the highest quality. Yet the whole question of quality and standards in the biofeedback field remains uncertain. The next year of research and treatment will be as exciting as past years, but serious questions have arisen about certain commercial firms and training procedures now being employed. While we want to maintain the investiga-

---

*Miller, in *Comprehensive Textbook of Psychiatry,* p. 360.
† Ibid., p. 359.

tory spirit, there must be guidelines and legal precedents to help stop the flagrant abuses that are going on. Many cases have been reported of biofeedback treatment that proved useless because treatment was conducted with unreliable equipment and/or untrained personnel.

Recently a woman called me to ask about treatment for her migraines. I informed her that I use biofeedback for treating these headaches. She told me she had already tried biofeedback. She had gone to a commercial firm that offered biofeedback, meditation, and mind training. They had hooked her up to an EEG (electroencephalograph), yet, to my knowledge, there is no evidence or indication that the brain-wave training can relieve migraines. The woman appears to have wasted her time and money.

Not too long ago in the American Medical Association newspaper, Dr. Bertram Brown, director of the National Institutes of Mental Health, issued guidelines for the use of behavior modification techniques, saying that such techniques were valuable in many cases but that they must be used with caution. He stated that "as many as 60,000 people are being treated by behavior modification techniques, but many of the therapists using them are 'outright quacks.'" A similar situation exists with biofeedback.

This problem of unlicensed therapists exists in all these new fields—biofeedback, behavior modification, and sex therapy. In New York State, for example, anyone can buy equipment and try to train, treat, or educate another person. Many of these unlicensed people are well intentioned—but would you want an untrained mechanic to repair the jet plane on which you were going to fly? It seems to be time for us to set standards and minimum qualifications for those who are giving biofeedback training, as well as for other kinds of therapists.

What can you do yourself to check a treatment center? First, ask if you will be treated by or under the supervision of a physician. If not, ask about the training and qualifications of the person who will treat you. Ask if there is any insurance covering your treatment or the person treating you. (Insurance is one legal measure that implies liability.) Also, ask how much EEG training they do and for what conditions. This will tell you a great deal about how they operate. If they indicate EEG as a clinical treatment for anything other than relaxation, ask them for the titles of published papers concerning this treatment, and ask if their use of EEG is clinical treatment or experimental work. Also, ask what the treatment results are. If they are at 30 percent (placebo level), you should look for better-trained therapists.

If you have further questions, get in touch with your local medical society or write to the Biofeedback Research Society, University of Colorado Medical Center, 4200 East Ninth Avenue, Denver, Colorado 80220. Those living in the metropolitan New York area may write to me care of St. Luke's Hospital, 114th Street and Amsterdam Avenue, New York City, New York 11025.

10.
A Biofeedback Experiment

Matthew J. Culligan

There has been some justifiable alarm concerning biofeedback machinery. So great are the need and hope on the part of the public for peace of mind, tranquility, happiness, or just plain relief from tension that rip-off artists have rushed into the field, knowing they can exploit people's longing for an easy way to find happiness. Not only has inferior equipment been sold, but experimental machinery has been touted as being capable of doing things it cannot do. Faddists and charlatans have already fleeced the public of hundreds of thousands of dollars, not to mention the severe damage that may have been done to the psyches of the individuals involved.

Biofeedback technology seems fated to go through the typical competitive enterprise cycle of too much, too soon, collapse and concentration, then domination by several large companies.

At the Stress Transformation Center we protected our trainees by working first only through doctor referrals. As word of mouth led to nondoctor inquiries, Dr. Sedlacek helped us screen patients. We introduced our first-time visitors to biofeedback machinery with a simple, inexpensive thermometer held between the thumb and first two fingers of either hand.

Because of the newness of the relationship, the decor of the center, and the natural shyness of most people, the skin temperature would usually register at between 78 and 83 degrees, though the body temperature was 98.6 degrees and the hand temperature of a relaxed person is usually around 85 to 90 degrees. The reason was simple: the slight stress of the meeting caused the blood to retreat to the heart, lung, and brain areas, with an attendant drop in the temperature at the extremities.

As the visitor listened, talked, and was impressed by the friendliness and dedication of the staff, the blood would begin to flow normally, and the thermometer would show a 1- or 2-degree rise. That usually broke the ice (pun intended), and this small accomplishment was the beginning of credibility for the center and biofeedback.

The GSR (galvanic skin response) unit was then demonstrated to the trainee. This small unit, created in the 19th century by Dr. Galvani and now transistorized, could be set to reflect the conductivity of the skin by measuring the amount of its moisture (perspiration). The unit would emit a sound whose pitch indicated the amount of moisture being produced.

As the visitor relaxed, the moisture decreased, and the sound lowered in pitch. That was a biofeedback reward for the trainee. The notion was reinforced by the staff member, who, when the GSR level was stabilized, would ask, "Do you mind if I stick this pin in your leg?" or to a trainee of the opposite sex, "Do you mind if I pinch you?" In the face of this threat, the pitch would rise within approximately two seconds, generally proving the point (again, pun intended).

More sophisticated equipment was also available and used to treat specific ailments. Most of the people who came to the center were helped, but after two years of not making even a modest profit, I realized that we had to try to go from a one-to-one treatment to working with large groups, as EST and TM are doing. I decided, in line with this, to see if biofeedback would have an application for corporations.

I went to the most conservative and traditional sector of U.S. business—the accounting profession—and selected a company to which to make my proposal. My choice, Haskins and Sells, is one of the largest certified public accounting firms in the country. I arranged a meeting with their management and outlined my program. What I told them in essence was that their executives and employees were their greatest assets and that if they were distress-free, they would not only function better, but they would tend to be more loyal and conscientious. They readily agreed to the experiment.

Five top-flight executives were chosen by management, and we put them through an eighteen-hour program that spanned three weeks. Our charge to Haskins and Sells was based on this time schedule and the use of relatively simple and inexpensive machinery: thermisters, GSRs, and a small EEG.

Shortly after the deal was made, the head of staff at the Stress Transformation Center told me about some EEG research involving a more sophisticated machinery setup that he felt would make this pilot program with Haskins and Sells a certain success. His argument was persuasive, and I agreed to meet the researcher involved and then make up my mind.

A meeting was set up, to take place in the researcher's laboratory.

The work was set up in a simple, functional

suite of offices, in which a modular setup of EEG machines were hooked up to oscilloscopes. The electrodes could be placed on the surface of the head in seven places, and the readings of the brain waves showed simultaneously on the oscilloscope screens. The electrodes and sound receivers were in another room, with a videotape camera directed at the subject. The viewer for that camera was in the researcher's office. The net effect was that he could wire up, talk to, and see the subject. Thus he could simultaneously evaluate the results of what he said and the brain-wave pattern of the subject.

The researcher gave me a quick briefing and sat me in the chair. He affixed the electrodes to my head, connected the mike and speaker to me, indicated the videotape camera pointed at me, told me to wait a moment, and left. The red light on the camera blinked on, beeping sounds entered the earpiece I was wearing, and my brain-wave testing began.

I started deep, rhythmic abdominal breathing, trying to clear my mind of all thoughts except of waves rolling in on an ocean beachfront. That had for decades been the mental picture that brought me peace of mind. The researcher said, "Not bad," and explained my reward, interesting-sounding electronic blips in sequence, indicating that my brain was in the alpha state. The sequences got more frequent and continuous, and I experienced great pleasure in hearing them. He then asked me if I could stop the blips for five seconds every minute or so. I was able to do this.

He then asked how I had done so well. I explained that as a youngster I would sit by myself on the boardwalk at Belle Harbor, Long Island, and actually watch the Atlantic waves roll in, absolutely loving the sight and sound. While I talked, the alpha waves stopped.

I was then asked to try other mental pictures, some with less motion. I tried a clear, unruffled lake; the alpha wave sounds came on strong. I tried others; then for an unknown reason, I adopted a mental picture of the scene that Michelangelo had painted on the ceiling of the Sistine Chapel in Rome, of God pointing to man. The researcher said, "Great, hold it!" The blips came on, strong and continuous.

The researcher didn't say a word. He didn't have to; we both knew something special had happened. He left me alone for many minutes, then quietly said, "Enough, Joe?" I said yes, was unhooked, and came out. We looked at each other silently for a while. Then he said with a smile, "You felt pretty good, eh?" I realized that I was calmer, happier, more rested than I could recall. I said, "This may get me back to church."

When I explained my final picture, he nodded and said, "That could be the reason for the extraordinary phasing of the brain waves. In all the others your creative brain was putting out strong waves of good volume and symmetry [he pointed these out on the graph], but the waves of your administrative brain increased." He pointed again to the long graph showing all the waves in synchronization. "Your whole brain was in phase."

I was so impressed by this demonstration that I agreed to let this new bit of machinery be used in the Haskins and Sells project even though the bill would be $15,000 greater. This meant that instead of turning a small profit for the project, we "lost our ass" as our accountant so elegantly put it, but I felt that if the project worked, we could sustain a loss because of the long-term gains it promised.

The results of the project, unhappily, were inconclusive. Of the five executives, three showed improvement: one quit smoking, another lost weight, and one increased his attention span. Of the other two, one didn't show up for enough sessions (a continual problem we hadn't counted on was arranging a time when all five men were free), and the other showed no change. It was unfortunate that we got carried away with the expensive machinery, because the sophisticated EEG did not add much to the project (and, indeed, as Dr. Sedlacek pointed out, there is no evidence as yet that the EEG is clinically helpful in the treatment of any disease). Perhaps if we had stuck to our modest initial plan, we might have been encouraged to try more of these needed projects. But maybe our experience will help others to avoid the pitfalls we experienced and mistakes we made and help to bring an industrial biofeedback program to large groups of workers.

Not long after the project, we decided to close the center. My head of staff, who was so talented and able at getting people to relax and work with the biofeedback treatment was not experienced enough in matters of profit and loss, which unfortunately was essential to keeping our operation going. (He has since been instrumental in bringing "mood rings" to the attention of the public. The rings, which employ quartz crystals in which heat-responsive chemicals are imprisoned, work solely on skin temperature. At about 90 degrees the stone is deep blue. As the temperature drops, the color changes to green, orange, gray, and finally to brown or black. The ring's value is that it indicates, as it goes from blue to brown or black, when you are experiencing increasing tension or flight or fight reactions. It does not as advertised indicate moods such as happiness or sadness. Unhappily, advertising has again attempted to oversell a basically good concept.)

Looking back on the experience, the one thing that I gained from the EEG session was the notion that I did have some control over my brain waves. I had grown up and matured as an adult believing that my body was controlled by my brain. That apparently was not true. Which leaves me with the question of what part of me is the control center? Could the soul be this something?

It seems that we are getting into more here than simply gaining greater knowledge about how the body operates. Philosophical and theological questions are also arising, which is as it should be, since we don't want to forget people in this equation. A kind word, a soft touch, and the appreciated response they bring are an essential, though different, kind of feedback. It is important that we recognize that machines have a place in our world as long as they don't become more important than people. I recall an argument between a computer expert, who was unalterably committed to the idea that the only way to measure the world was by numbers, and who was devastated by an Irish poet's question, "How would you measure the smile of a child?"

11.
Five Simple Steps to Controlling Distress

Keith Sedlacek, M.D.

If you have been reading between the lines thus far, I don't think I even have to point out that I feel (along with a growing number of medical and psychiatric professionals) that the mind and the body are so intimately linked in the health of the individual that the two cannot be separated. This increasing awareness is the reason why more and more therapies are involved with exercising the body as well as working with the mind.

Exercise is of paramount importance to our bodies. Without it our muscles would atrophy (grow smaller). Atrophy is usually brought about through disuse or injury (where the nerve has been diseased, damaged, or cut and cannot activate or contract the muscles). Either of these situations is a serious blow to the health of the body and, increasingly, we suspect, to the mind.

Two of our greatest protections against disease are proper diet and regular exercise. For this and other reasons, many doctors are strongly recommending that their patients have a daily physical workout. One of the greatest benefits of exercise is the unique relaxation that comes in its aftermath—a sense of relaxation that cannot be duplicated artificially.

Dr. Edward Greenwood, a psychiatrist at the

Menninger Clinic, feels that exercise provides a ready source of emotional well-being.

In fact, the benefits of physical exercise range from an acceptable means of resolving frustration and relieving boredom to strengthening the ego and sublimating aggressive drives. Dr. Greenwood goes on to say that "unfortunately we have allowed a man's worth to be measured according to his material accumulation, his bank balance, his investments, his home, cars, boats, and power equipment. Rarely do we look to see how complete the individual is. What he does to his body on the way toward achieving his stockpile seems immaterial."

Things are changing and "recreational therapy, including pure physical exercise, has long been an adjunct to psychiatric treatment. Now with the growing emphasis on preventive medicine, recreational therapy has come more and more into its own."* Physical exercise, Dr. Greenwood feels, helps develop a strong and constructive ego.

Through exercise, the sublimation of aggressive drives also becomes possible. The pent-up anger and hostility that can eat holes in our stomach linings and make ugly human beings of us find a direct and socially acceptable outlet on the golf course, tennis court, or at the gym.

I play tennis and basketball, and take dance classes. I also exercise for fifteen minutes each day and maintain a weight within ten pounds of my ideal high school weight. Everyone should strive to stay within ten pounds of their high school weight unless, of course, you were overweight or under-

---

*E. Greenwood, in *American Medical News*, June 23-30, 1975, p. 19.

weight then. The ideal strategy is to exercise each day for fifteen minutes and then to plan two to three one-half to one-hour sessions of active exercise (such as swimming, running, and tennis) per week. Swimming is particularly good in that it makes equal use of almost all our muscles. At St. Luke's Hospital, all five of my psychiatric supervisors regularly engage in either one or a combination of the following: tennis, swimming, dance, sailing and boating.

Besides exercise, we're finding that people's attitudes have a lot to do with the events of their lives. In biofeedback, the patient's attitude is critical. Those who believe they cannot influence their bodies and minds for personal good health will continue to experience poor health.

Those who can use the powerful techniques and sensitive instruments of biofeedback by imagining and "seeing" the results help the process immeasurably. At first they make small changes, and then with a mental image that works for them, as demonstrated by the feedback, they rapidly gain self-control.

Each morning you should picture how you would like the day to go. Visualize the day and plan to take some time for your enjoyment: to read, play, talk. Imagine some pleasant scenes, and do your best during the day to allow the good things to happen. Take interest in and learn from the "bad things" that come your way. They are also valuable learning experiences.

Do not waste time by reacting to other people when there is no opportunity for change or exchange. Use your intelligence to develop as much as possible a healthy cortex-autonomic system. If an emergency arises, you are prepared (particularly if you exercise) to handle it automatically (or, shall we say, autonomically).

Do not blow your top over traffic jams. Listen to music, talk, or do simple relaxation exercises while you wait for the traffic to move. Carry a book with you and read when you might have to do some waiting in other places.

Listed below are five steps that, if followed for only ten to fourteen days, will help get you started on rebalancing your autonomic system and will give you a sense of better health and vitality. Continued daily use of these steps will be of major help in dealing with the harmful effects of stress.

Step 1: Exercise on an empty stomach for five to fifteen minutes after getting up in the morning. Include stretches for the arms, legs, stomach, and back, and some favorite physical movements. Hatha yoga has many simple exercises, such as "welcoming the sun," that provide exercise for all of your muscles. Other exercises such as knee bends, touching your toes, and the Royal Canadian Air Force exercises are also helpful. Ballet stretches and exercises are good, or you might like to shadowbox or jog in place for two to four minutes. It is important that you stretch all the muscles and get the heart pumping blood. You should have worked up a light sweat if you have exercised sufficiently. (A yearly physical examination is imperative, and you should also have an exam before you embark on any new exercise plan or diet.)

Step 2: Step 2 is divided into two parts. First take fifteen to twenty minutes to practice the "relaxation response"; it consists of a mental device—a passive attitude, decreased muscle tension, and a quiet environment. To elicit this response, Dr. Benson* suggests that you sit or lie in a comfortable chair or bed in a quiet environment. Close your eyes and deeply relax all your muscles, beginning with the toes and progressing up to the thighs to the stomach, chest, arms, shoulders, neck, face, and head. Breathe out through your nose and become aware of your breathing. Say the word "one" each time you breathe out. Continue this practice for fifteen to twenty minutes. At first you may need to check the time, but you will soon be able to gauge it yourself. After you finish, simply sit or lie quietly for a minute or two. Then open your eyes gently and get up when you are ready. You should not practice within two hours after a meal. Do not try to force or strain or make the relaxation happen; simply maintain attention during the relaxation. With the first few practice sessions you will start to experience a deeper relaxation. Your limbs will start to feel heavy and you may experience warmth, tingling, and other sensations in your body.

How does this work? Along with the flight or fight response (or egotropic response), there is a relaxation response (or trophotropic response). This response was described by Hess [†] in his experiments on the brain of a cat. The response starts in the hypothalamus. Activation of a particular zone in the hypothalamus results in a generalized decrease in the activity of the sympathetic nervous system and

---

*H. Benson, "Your Innate Asset for Combating Stress," *Harvard Business Review,* July-August 1974.
†W. Hess, *Functional Organization of the Diencephalon.* New York, Grune & Stratton, 1957.

a possible increase in parasympathetic activity.* Thus, if this zone is electrically stimulated, the result is a decrease in blood pressure, a decreased respiratory rate, and pupil constriction—the opposite of the flight or fight response.

The relaxation response exercise brings about a relaxed physiological state which is also seen in some meditative states. In effect, it allows the body a period of readjustment, of low arousal, and of relaxation.

In the second part of Step 2, after practicing the relaxation response, simply imagine for one or two minutes the day going the way you would like it to. Imagine yourself being confident and enjoying the events of the day. Picture these activities and then begin your day.

Step 3: Take another fifteen to twenty minutes and practice the relaxation response again. My patients often practice this relaxation exercise twice a day, as well as doing more sophisticated exercises (one of which I will give later in the chapter) that I teach them during their training. The times when they prefer to use the relaxation response are at work, after work, or before going to bed. On a particularly stressful day, they may slip in a third short session. You should not do more than two or three sessions a day, because these "rest periods" should not become an excuse to hide from work or relationships. What I am suggesting is not withdrawal but reenergizing and relaxing.

My recommendation is that you do Step 3 in the evening or before bed. This is because you should do

*H. Benson, et al., "The Relaxation Response," *Psychiatry,* vol. 37, February 1974, p. 37.

at least five minutes of relaxation before Step 4, and some people like to do Steps 3 and 4 one after the other.

Step 4: Dr. Stroebel calls this the daily review. After at least five minutes of relaxing, so that your body is in a relaxed state, simply review the day in your mind. You should review your day as if it were a moving picture, except that you run it in reverse. This allows you to examine the pattern and flow of the day. You can see when and under what conditions you were stressed and how you reacted. You will also recall the situations and feelings surrounding the times when you were relaxed and when you were tense. This will allow you, in a relaxed state, to notice little habits and patterns that escaped you before. In this way you can learn to identify your stressors and the sources of time pressure, and the conditions under which the pressures and stresses are worse. Then you can take steps to alleviate them or to change the situation. This review exercise has proved to be very helpful to my patients, and Dr. Stroebel has used it for hundreds of patients.

During this time you must learn to be an objective observer of your day's events. This is a specific learning experience. If you find yourself being overcritical, depressed, or highly elated over the day's events, you should seek aid in one of two places. First see if you can share these incidents with a friend. If your friend can't offer you any perspective, or if you find you can't speak openly with him or her, you should seek professional aid, because your tendency in reviewing your day is to be overly involved and possibly neurotic. The purpose of this daily review is to help you recognize your patterns of dealing with stress (life) and to be gentle with yourself. There is no reason to punish yourself or to strain too hard, toward sadness or happiness, in these mental and physical exercises.

Step 5: Set aside two 45-minute periods each week during which you do some strenuous physical activity, such as jogging, playing tennis or squash, swimming, doing yoga or dance movements, or even taking a brisk walk. Notice how you feel at the end of this activity. Discover the difference between mental and physical tiredness and how good the body can feel after such bodily exertion.

If on a particular day you discover that you do not have enough time to do Steps 1 and 2 thoroughly, do just a few stretching exercises and ten minutes of the relaxation response, but do not eliminate either step. What is important is that you do these exercises daily. If you skip them for a day or more, you are cheating your body of the time it needs to relax. After you become adept at doing the steps, you will find that you can rapidly move into deeper states of relaxation. Consequently, if you are rushed, you can shorten the time and still treat your body to considerable relaxation. Once you have gotten into the routine of these steps, I feel you will enjoy the physical relaxation and mental quietness so much that you will not want to shorten the time.

For those who are curious about the exercises I give my patients, here is one of the first sets I start them on. These exercises are both physical and mental. Similar exercises are done in progressive relaxation and yoga.

Dr. Sedlacek's Anti-Stress Exercises

First, stand upright and simply drop your head forward toward your chest. Then, imagining that the top of your head is leading your head around, start to move your head in a full circle. Do the exercise three times clockwise and then three times counterclockwise. This will loosen the neck muscles and help relax the face. Next, clasp your hands by intertwining your fingers behind you and turn the clasped palms downward. Extend the clasped hands back and out as far as possible, lean all the way forward from the waist and keep the clasped hands up as high as possible, with the palms now facing the ceiling or sky (these exercises are particularly wonderful when done outside in pleasant surroundings). Hold the arms extended for eight to ten seconds, and then drop the hands so that now both your hands and head hang in front of you. You may keep your knees straight or let them bend slightly. Just hang there for a four- or five-second count.

Now straighten up slowly, lifting from your buttocks and lower back. Try to imagine each vertebra in the spine slowly straightening up—starting from the pelvis, gradually raising the lower back, upper back, neck, and finally the head and coming to rest comfortably in a vertical position. With your feet 2 to 4 inches apart, again clasp your hands, palms downward, behind you. Bend your head forward, and keeping your knees straight, slip your hands down toward your knees or, if possible, to your ankles. (Again don't strain too hard; you will be able to move closer to the ankles each day. If you only reach your lower thighs, that's okay. The idea is to start stretching the back and spine comfortably.) When you have gone as low as you can, simply breathe in and out four or five times and feel the tension in the back and legs. Then let the hands unclasp and again slowly straighten up, one vertebra at a time.

If you have back difficulties, or if you find these exercises too painful, do not do them without a doctor's supervision. Consult your doctor if you have any doubts about your ability to do them. I tell all my patients that these exercises are not meant to cause pain but to cause relaxation through stretching and increasing suppleness.

In the second part of my exercise program, you lie on your back on a firm surface such as a hard floor with a ¼- to ½-inch-thick rug covering it. Do not do these exercises on a mattress or sofa, because a certain firmness is necessary. A rug or two or three blankets underneath you should provide enough comfort. Place your palms about 5 to 7 inches from your hips and face them up toward the ceiling or sky. Push the heels of your feet out and then relax them. Wiggle your head up and down and to the right and the left. Then let the head rest on the floor, facing up.

Now close your eyes and try breathing in the following manner. Inhale through the nose to the count of three, pause for count of three, exhale again through the nose to a count of three and pause for a count of three. Repeat, and soon you will not need to count out the intervals. Be sure to pause between breathing in and out. After some practice, you can use a count of four for the breathing. Do this three or four times. Then, breathing normally, clench your right hand into a fist. Try to feel the tension in the fist and forearm. It is okay if the muscles tremble. After a count of twelve to fifteen, relax the fist and feel the difference as the forearm, hand, and fingers relax. Try to feel the relaxation flowing into the forearm, hand, and fingers. Breathe slowly three or four times and then repeat with the left hand.

After three or four slow breaths, clench both the left and right hands into fists for a count of fifteen and be aware of the tension in both hands. Then relax again more deeply, noticing the difference between the feeling of tension and the feeling of relaxation.

After three or four slow breaths, focus on your face. Simply frown and tense up the forehead tighter and tighter. Feel the tension for a count of twelve to fifteen, and then relax the muscles and imagine the forehead as relaxed as possible. After each tensing, relax and breathe slowly three or four times.

Now tighten the muscles around the eyes and feel the tension. Relax, breathe, and then clamp your teeth together and feel that tension. Note how strong these muscles are, and then relax and breathe slowly three or four times.

Now let the entire face relax: the forehead, the eyes, the nose, the cheeks, the mouth, and chin. Try to enjoy the relaxation—allow yourself to relax more and more. Breathe slowly three or four times.

Now pull your shoulders up toward the head. Imagine that the tops of your shoulders are going to reach up to touch your ears. Be aware of the tension for a count of fifteen. Try to keep the rest of the body relaxed while the shoulders are tensed. Now relax the shoulders and let the relaxation flow down from the relaxed face into the shoulders and down to the arms to the very tips of your fingers. Breathe slowly three or four times.

Take a deep breath and hold it for ten seconds. Notice the tension in the chest and then breathe out. Let yourself breathe freely and easily, allowing the chest wall to move in and out. Allow yourself to relax more with each exhalation.

Breathe slowly four or five times, noticing and enjoying the relaxation. Now tighten the buttocks and legs. With these muscles tightened, push the toes down and away from your face and trunk, and feel the tension in your toes, ankles, and calf muscles. Hold this tension for ten seconds and then relax. Pull the toes up toward your face for ten seconds. Then relax completely.

In your mind imagine yourself relaxing the face ... neck ... arms ... chest ... back ... stomach ... thighs ... knees ... ankles ... and feet ... all relaxing. Readjust your body to relieve any tension spots you may have noticed.

In your mind imagine a wave of relaxation starting from the top of your head and sweeping down the body, relaxing your whole body more and more. Follow this wave of relaxation as it washes over all the parts of your body, until it finally reaches your toes. Imagine all the tension just streaming out of your toes into the air and sky.

Spend the next ten minutes just breathing and listening to your breath. If any bothersome thoughts come into your mind, say the word "one," each time you exhale, just as in the relaxation response, and these thoughts will leave.

This set of exercises may replace the first of the two relaxation responses. Either will give you generalized relaxation, but I feel that the muscle tensing and relaxing will allow you to tune in on the tension you may not be aware of normally.

The steps and the exercises offered here require about one hour of your entire day. In return for this investment, you will experience greater bodily vigor and mental clarity after just one or two weeks. If you say you cannot spare this time, be sure you are willing to take responsibility for the fact that you are a partner in maintaining your distress (or disease, if it has gotten that far). By putting this information to work, you can give your body at least some period of relief from distress each day. As you practice these exercises every day, you soon will start to bring about deep relaxation just by breathing. As I have suggested—breathe in for a count of three, pause three, breathe out three, pause three. There is no better time than now to begin to help the mind and body to work cooperatively for mental and physical health.

Remember the five steps:

1. Exercise for five to fifteen minutes each morning.

2. Practice the relaxation response for fifteen to twenty minutes (or do the set of exercises just described), and then imagine, for one to two minutes, the day going well for you.

3. Practice the relaxation response a second time during the day or before bedtime.

4. Do your daily review after at least five minutes of relaxation.

5. Set aside two 45-minute periods each week for some strenuous physical activity.

These five steps are not a treatment for any particular diseases or ailment unless specifically prescribed by a doctor. They are suggestions, and, like the others outlined in this book, they will help you to deal better with stress. Practiced every day, they will help you to decrease the negative effects of stress in your everyday life and provide you with a sense of a calmer, healthier you.

12.
My Personal Program for Fitness and Health

Matthew J. Culligan

Up to this point, Dr. Sedlacek and I have tried, and we hope we have been successful, to convince you not only that stress is a condition, indeed a requirement, for life but that you can learn to control it. Without stress, a body is lifeless. The light and constructive side of stress is positive energy. The dark and deadly side is distress. That knowledge alone can be helpful, but it is only the beginning. Never was the statement "A little knowledge is a dangerous thing" truer. We must go beyond this knowledge and incorporate the information presented here until it becomes second nature to us. We must truly understand ourselves and our bodies.

In this era of shortages of power and raw materials, it is too easy to forget that the human race has one unlimited resource: human imagination. Imagination gives rise to philosophical as well as innovative thinking. When what you know is supplemented by imagination and "processed" in your mental computer, the beautiful result is understanding. But even understanding is not enough; the ideal is the further step of making a commitment to act positively on this understanding.

We trust you have found the preceding pages informative, instructive, and worthy of consideration. The remaining chapters look ahead, and we will not concentrate on distress any further. We urge you to set all your thoughts to positive energy.

We will present techniques for achieving positive energy chronologically for the very good reason that every day you will *be* what your picture of yourself is when you start out the day. Logic dictates, therefore, that you do whatever you can to start out each day with a positive picture of yourself. Something *may* happen during any day to change that picture, but if your mental picture is habitually strong, you will be highly resistant to hostile words, acts, or circumstances.

As you may know by now, sports play a big part in Dr. Sedlacek's and my life. We encourage everyone to become involved in some sport because it is the most painless way to get in the exercise we all need regularly. Every sport seems to work its own magic on the participants. Golf is superb because before you can master the game, you must learn to master yourself. Tennis has the advantage of enabling a player to get a great workout in an hour or less. It demands full attention as well.

Horseback riding, a particular favorite of mine, was best described by a contemporary of Teddy Roosevelt who said: "There is nothing as good for the inside of a man as the outside of a horse." This sport is also very absorbing because you must keep your wits about you if you don't want to get your neck broken. Most horses are slow-witted, capable of killing themselves and you, unless you are in charge of the situation. Despite the potential danger, horse riding is superb for children. Rarely will you find or hear of youngsters getting into trouble who are absorbed in the training, schooling, and showing of horses. Volleyball is a lovely group sport that provides plenty of exercise. (I must admit to having a mad passion for seeing it played by mixed male and female teams, nude.)

For me, though I enjoy golf enormously, swimming is my all-time favorite, in terms of the conversion of distress into positive energy. Over the years, I've tried to figure out why. I am satisfied with some of the apparent reasons. First, the total immersion is an incomparable overall sensation. Second, the chilliness of the water (unless you are someplace where it is warm all the time) drives out all thoughts other than "Christ, it's cold!" Then there is the rhythmical breathing that is known to be relaxing. Because of the weightlessness there is little heart strain and it is very difficult to overdo swimming. There must be some psychological lift, perhaps having to do with the well-supported theory that our ancestors slithered out of the water eons ago and the fact that we all spend nine months in our mother's amneotic fluid (that protective water in the womb). Water play, particularly with children, greatly relieves distress and often can provide that incomparably good feeling of physical tiredness.

During my worst days, living a pressure-cooker life, swimming became almost an obsession. I'd start thinking about the pool an hour from home. The simple process of thinking about it relieved some of the tension. I'd drive directly to the pool cabana, shuck my clothes and leap into the water that came from a 200-foot-deep well warmed only, to the dismay of my family, by the sun.

The rest of this chapter is devoted to my suggestions for handling stress and getting the most out of life. They work for me. They may work for you if we share physical and psychological traits and are on the same biological timeclock. That is a key factor. Humans do vary in terms of their biological makeup. For example, I need very little sleep at night, but I take frequent naps for rest and fresh energy—five to six 5-minute breaks a day. If you *need* eight hours of uninterrupted sleep nightly, you will want to make appropriate modifications of my regimen and rules, which are:

1. Do not stay in bed in the morning unless you are sleeping. Unless I can go back to sleep immediately, I get up no matter what time I awaken. I exercise, read, or write. Occasionally after one of those activities I feel drowsy and return to sleep.

2. Do some exercise every morning; particularly to keep your waistline trim. This is a morale-builder, particularly if you can keep your waistline trim. It is also a necessity if you hope to maintain optimal physical and mental well-being.

3. Shower every morning after exercise, first as hot as you can stand it, then as cold as possible. Establish a mental picture of how courageous and daring one must be to take this cold shower.

4. Eat a good, well-balanced breakfast. The ideal way to eat is a large, well-balanced breakfast, a small lunch, and a tiny dinner. Eating habits die slowly. Most people do the reverse: no breakfast, or just coffee (dreadful), a full lunch, and a huge dinner. If those who follow this mode are sedentary after dinner, the effects on their weight and health can be disastrous.

5. Practice a light exercise routine well after dinner or before retiring. I walk from one to three miles after dinner, stopping occasionally to see a good movie.

6. If you are very busy, make a list each evening of things that must be done the next day, and a list of what should be done if possible. Concentrate on the former, and don't be distracted by the latter until you have done all you can about the items on the first list. Only then should you tackle the latter. You'll be surprised to find how well you do on the first list if you are not distracted; also you'll find some problems on the second list will disappear or lose priority simply by being left alone.

7. Try to pause for momentary reflection if someone offends, insults, or irritates you. If the driver of another car cuts you off or drives recklessly, remember that he has a problem—he will probably be a statistic one day. If you receive an insult, remember that the person insulting you is either wrong or right. If he's wrong, *he* has a problem. Why should you involve yourself in someone else's problem? If he's right, consider the insult a favor, and do something about the fault.

8. Don't fly off the handle. When you do, it is a sign of lack of control of the autonomic nervous system. That is, you are reacting violently and without thinking to an outside barb. Sometimes this kind of release if good, but, in the main, it is an overreaction and can be prevented by a moment of reflection.

9. Have your blood pressure checked regularly. If there is any hereditary tendency toward stroke, heart condition, kidney disease, or premature death

in your family, have your blood pressure checked every three months. The day may come when biofeedback devices can be worn on the hands and wrists to act as early warning indicators of high blood pressure, but right now it takes only thirty seconds for your doctor to check your blood pressure.

10. Try to develop your own code of morals and ethics to personalize, supplement, or replace the codes that have proved insufficient for you. Decide what *you* will and will not do, and reduce your concern over what others do and do not do. Allow others the room to do what they want to do.

11..Rout feelings of guilt implanted during your youth by the rules of others. The rest of your life starts in the next minute. Why drag old guilt feelings into that atmosphere, which can be as clean as you make it? In particular, don't feel guilty because you live while others died horribly (I address this to Jews, specifically, who may feel this kind of guilt in relation to those who perished in the Holocaust). Don't feel guilty about your children's failings if you did the best you knew how to do when they were young. You were growing up then, too, you know. If you've lost contact with your children, why not call or write? Tell them that you love them and that you'll be there if they need you. You'll be amazed at how relieved you'll feel by just saying it, and you might be startled by the response.

12. Memorize or keep handy some words which inspire you. These, of Winston Churchill, to the vanquished, humiliated people of France, never fail to move me:

> Goodnight, then: Sleep to gather strength for the morning, for the morning will come. Brightly will it

shine on the brave and true, the kindly and all who suffer for the cause, and gloriously on the tombs of heroes. Thus will shine the dawn.

13. When problems mount, and death, divorce, illness, job loss, and other problems seem to threaten your sanity, balance, and health, *do something.* Do anything, but don't sit and moan. Walk, jog, swim, soak in a tub, take a sauna, see a movie, flirt, make love, eat, read, argue, telephone your friends, and *talk.* Talk a mile a minute, but talk. Talk in itself is therapeutic. Cry if you can, but keep moving physically, emotionally, and spiritually. Try to realize through all adversity that it is in these times that we learn and grow. See if you can discern what the lessons are in trying circumstances.

13.
The Individual, Society, and Disease Prevention

Matthew J. Culligan and Keith Sedlacek, M.D.

For this final chapter, we are departing from our practice of individual presentation to speak together as one. In the months it took to write this book we have come to realize that we have reached higher levels of thought together than we could have reached individually. Our relationship has been a classic example of cerebral and emotional feedback. We have learned a great deal from each other.

A key phrase in our learning experience has been *to relate*. In particular we have tried to teach you to relate to the stress around you and how it affects your body. Forewarned is forearmed.

All creatures must learn to relate. The living cell that can't adjust to its environment must die, just as species of animals became extinct when they could no longer adapt to the conditions in which they found themselves. Humans survived into the twentieth century by relating to the earth's environment: by recognizing the effects of the elements and coming to terms with the other inhabitants of the planet. But by the time of the Industrial Revolution, it was becoming evident that some people had ceased to relate to the earth's environment and were trying to dominate it.

These people, despite their towering achievements in production, transportation, distribution, and marketing, left "time bombs" all over our landscape. The explosion of these time bombs is an increasing cause of much of the distress in contemporary life. The land was scourged, the forests stripped, the waters poisoned, the ignorant and the poor exploited, and the wealth controlled by a few. Politicians, lawyers, and accountants were corrupted, officials bribed, and the first commandment became: "Get thine first." The second was: "It's okay as long as you don't get caught." As this philosophy increased, people not only turned against their environment but against themselves. Intelligence agencies instituted the keeping of files, and soon there were dossiers on anyone who spoke out or questioned the direction our nation was taking.

When the distressful events got so bad that we could no longer turn away, we began looking at ourselves, realizing that a change of consciousness was needed and that it must begin within.

If we can begin to see ourselves differently, perhaps we can move from there to seeing others differently. If we can develop our own self-worth, surely we will be able to recognize it in others.

We will not presume to give you specific advice in the area of spirituality or humanism, but we will strive to contribute to your physical and mental well-being by helping you to increase your endurance and vitality. We believe your endurance and vitality will be in direct proportion to (1) your understanding of stress, (2) your desire to power your days with positive energy, and (3) your ability to avoid distress by practicing our stress management steps.

We trust that having read this far, your understanding of stress and distress has grown considerably. It cannot be overemphasized how crucial your picture of yourself is. You can power your days with positive energy by mentally creating and holding a positive picture of yourself at the beginning of each day. With a negative picture, you will have the feeling that everyone and everything is against you. In fact, the people we meet are simply responding (consciously or subconsciously) to our attitude.

Your attitude, of course, will depend upon your own self-esteem. Your uniqueness is the foundation not of false pride, but of justifiable self-esteem. This self-esteem will be supported by your ability to manage distress and to keep yourself free to deal constructively with your life and its challenges.

If your self-esteem is at a high level, you will be able consciously to avoid habits that are destructive physically, emotionally, and mentally. Excessive eating and smoking, problem drinking, the use of mind-stultifying or mind-destroying drugs are virtual impossibilities, over a long period of time, for human beings who feel good about themselves.

Elimination of those destructive habits will add greatly to your stamina and vigor. If you can henceforth *override* the automatic stress responses as they occur, we believe that you will be on the road to maximum endurance and vitality.

Here is a technique, in addition to those we have already given, that will be helpful any time you feel yourself becoming excessively stressed. At the instant something threatening, irritating, or perplexing happens, take a deep breath, then exhale slowly and thoroughly. Let your neck muscles and shoulders relax or slump.

Standing or sitting erect, take a deep breath, counting to three as you inhale. Hold for a count of three, exhale to the count of three, and pause for a count of three. Then repeat. As you practice, you can increase the count to four. Do this every hour if you are tense, or at every instance of tension.

During these seconds you will be overriding the automatic flight or fight response, blocking the signals that would otherwise trigger the little chemical "guns" all over the body. As you repeat this breathing exercise, you will come to benefit from it almost instantly, because your body will "learn" to slow the overreaction of the fight or flight response. This will in no way hamper your power to react instantly to real physical danger. Obviously, if a car is bearing down on you, neither biofeedback, yoga, TM, or any other technique will be preferable to jumping for your life. (We are not suggesting that there will not be times when an aroused state will be absolutely appropriate. What we want to do is to teach you to turn it off when it may be harmful to you.)

Throughout this book we have tried to point out the interrelation of the mind and body with stress and disease. Initially most disease was thought to be organic or physical in origin. Consequently, the treatment encompassed physical methods of dealing with disease, and the particular choice of treatment was often based on the doctor's orientation or bias. If the doctor was trained in surgery, surgery was the first method used to deal with the disease. For example, one of the treatments for Raynaud's disease, in cases of severe pain, is to cut out the sympathetic nerve system to give relief. Surgery is an invaluable medical tool and continues to be a major form of healing and disease intervention, but it should be employed only as a last resort in stress-related diseases. At the other end of the spectrum, psychiatrists often prescribed lengthy analysis (sometimes running to ten years for many symptoms and diseases), with mixed results.

Recently, the most popular way of controlling disease has been through the use of medication. Hypertension, diabetes, and infections, for example, have been effectively controlled by this method. The problems with this form of treatment are that the drugs often produce side effects, they must be taken daily, and they can mask the cause of the distress. We are not suggesting that people stop taking the medication they need but that they realize they are paying a price for this form of treatment.

The least quantifiable way of treating disease has been that of the personal influence of the doctor on the patient through encouragement and reassurance to try to get patients to revise their life styles to control the ailment. This method is used by professionals ranging from psychotherapists to general practitioners.

It is only within the last one hundred years that we have come to realize that many ailments are primarily psychological, and not physical, in origin. One of the first to note this was Freud at the turn of the century when he began using psychotherapy to treat women for hysterical conversion (a condition of apparent paralysis) and effected a "cure." From that point on more and more diseases were suspected of being caused by the effects of the mind and not solely of the body.

The physical approach to medicine (surgery, medication, vitamins, x-rays) continued to dominate, however, because it could not only demonstrate and quantify its results, but its methods were often quicker. Consequently, the philosophy prevailed that the new physical problems, such as obesity, and the new epidemics, such as heart attacks, were caused by physical substances, for example, cholesterol. Yet the field of medicine has not stemmed the tide of the new epidemics.

One of the first breakthroughs away from this kind of thinking occurred when Masters and Johnson published their dramatic work on the treatment of sexual dysfunction (*Human Sexual Inadequacy,* Little, Brown, 1970). They showed that by working directly with the symptom and by using physical techniques and counseling to reshape behavior, they could eliminate an astonishing percentage of sexual difficulties (60 to 90 percent success rate for difficult problems such as premature ejaculation). Their course, which takes only two weeks, but includes five years of follow-up, has demonstrated the continuing effectiveness of the treatment. Masters and Johnson's work has demonstrated that specific short-term methods not only "cured" the symptoms but also helped to change other behavioral (sexual-social) patterns. Today most major medical centers not only use Masters and Johnson's techniques, but they also make certain that medical students are exposed to the widest possible training in regard to common sexual problems.

More recently, as mentioned earlier, Drs. Friedman and Rosenman have made a major contribution to medicine by pointing out that personality and behavior are the major causes of heart attacks and strokes. They made concrete suggestions as to how those with Type A behavior (those with the highest risk) could change their behavior patterns to reduce their chances of being stricken. There are now therapy groups in hospitals to assist people to start to change their Type A behavior.

What these two examples prove, we think, is that we mustn't get pigeonholed into one way of approaching healing. We must look at the total individual if we are to find the answer to what ails him or her. New discoveries are teaching us more and more about the nature of disease and its causes.

The burning question, of course, is, how can the individual and society lessen the disease and distress that are now so prevalent? Through primarily preventive steps we have eliminated many of the serious diseases, such as polio and typhoid fever. Now we seem to be faced with an epidemic of stress-related diseases: heart attacks, hypertension, diabetes, and perhaps even cancer.

We would like to suggest that preventive steps be taken for stress-related diseases as well. As we indicated earlier, measuring devices such as the Social Readjustment Scale may help us to predict which types of individuals have a high risk of contracting disease. These people, of course, should then begin to take preventive action. The earlier the intervention, the smaller the chances of distress and disease, and the milder the ailments if they do occur. Therefore, children and adolescents should be made aware of the effects of distress and of what they can do to relieve their bodies of this tension. Perhaps everyone should receive some preventive biofeedback training and exposure to the mental and physical exercises that they can use to relax their bodies. This kind of relaxation would, for those who practice it daily, interrupt their pattern of accumulated stress.

Other techniques are also being used to reduce stress. Specifically we will look at those currently enjoying enormous popularity—the relaxation response, transcendental meditation, and yoga. (Zen apparently also offers some techniques that quiet the mind and body, but these methods are not in wide use in this country and we are unfamiliar with them.)

The relaxation response was first formulated by Dr. Herbert Benson of the Harvard Medical School after he had tested the effectiveness of TM. He demonstrated that TM brought about specific physiological changes in the body, for example, an 18 to 20 percent decrease in oxygen consumption, and an increase in GSR, that were different from those that occurred during sleep. He now feels that a similar condition can be achieved by activating the relaxation response. Dr. Benson thinks that prayer and meditation during religious rituals probably brought about this decrease in the activity of the sympathetic system and thus served a greater function than the supplicant may have realized.

Dr. Benson is encouraging the use of the relaxation response to improve the general state of health, and he is examining its use in decreasing blood pressure and certain heartrate difficulties. He has published some first data that supports the response as a significant aid in these areas. The relaxation response can be learned easily and usually at no cost.

Transcendental meditation was introduced in the United States by Maharishi Mahesh Yogi, an Indian priest. It consists of two 15- to 20-minute periods of meditation per day in which a mantra is silently repeated. The mantra is one of seventeen

Sanskrit words, one of which is chosen and given to each individual. The mantra seems to have, as Drs. Gluck and Stroebel have demonstrated, the special quality of synergizing alpha waves in the brain after a minute or two, if regularly practiced for two to three months.*

At the time this book was written, the fee for the TM course was $125 for adults and $65 for students. TM is fast becoming a big business. The group is now incorporated and has started a university in Iowa. (Scientology, a quasi-religious group, was the first group to use a type of GSR in their therapy or desensitization process. The results of their work to my own knowledge have never been published.)

Various medical people other than Dr. Benson have experimented with TM. Drs. Gluck and Stroebel have suggested that TM is a helpful adjunct (along with psychotherapy and medication) in the treatment of mental patients. They report, however, that TM does not seem to be an effective treatment for specific ailments such as migraine headaches. While some patients get better because of the general relaxation, others may get worse.† Dr. Patricia Carrington at Princeton University is using TM techniques in psychotherapy and reports that their use speeds up therapy and is extremely helpful to the therapist and the patient.

TM is relatively easily taught and fairly inexpensive. It does appear to have a general calming effect that is reported to help to decrease the need for certain addictive drugs. It is currently en-

*B. Gluck and C. Stroebel, "Comprehensive Psychiatry." In F. Freyhan, ed., *Biofeedback and Meditation in the Treatment of Psychiatric Illness,* New York, Grune & Stratton, 1974.
† Ibid.

countering some of the problems all institutions have as it expands and proponents use big business techniques to sell the approach.

By far the oldest relaxation technique is yoga. It also evolved in India and consists of physical and meditative exercises. The usefulness of these exercises has been written about for years. Yoga exercises are generally inexpensive to learn and those who practice it daily report that minor ailments and distress are eased by it. Dr. Chandra Patel used yoga exercises and GSR feedback successfully in her treatment of hypertensive patients.*

What is noteworthy about all these techniques, including biofeedback, is that they require daily practice or the beneficial effects are lessened—often dramatically. Western medicine has been aware of the need for daily work in such areas as muscular rehabilitation, but the aspect of discipline has gotten lost or been replaced by the daily pill routine, which is seen most clearly in our dependence on substances such as Valium and Librium. All these techniques also appear to produce their general effect through the activation of the trophotropic (relaxation) zone.

Of course, each of these techniques differs from the others in some way. The relaxation response is the simplest, requiring no physical exercise; TM provides a similar state plus the effects of the mantra; and yoga offers both exercises and meditation Where all three of these fall down, in our opinion, is that to date none of them systematically provides supportive backup, discussion, or follow-up for all their clients. Biofeedback, when done under prope.

---

*C. Patel, "Twelve Months' Following of Yoga and Biofeedback in the Management of Hypertension," *Lancet,* January 11, 1975.

medical supervision, offers a scientific relaxation technique, specific therapy for specific diseases, plus further therapy when needed and regular follow-up.

The increasing popularity of all these techniques, plus their physical and mental effects, demonstrates that they are fulfilling a need. We would like to offer one cautionary note about the *sole* dependence on any technique that has its origins in religion or mysticism and implies a disregard for the physical body. While it might be helpful or necessary for some to lead the ascetic life, it does have its limitations for the general physical as well as mental health of people and society at large. As Pete Hamill recently wrote: "Religion has led to an incredible history of slaughter and destruction: mysticism with its insistence on passivity has led millions down the road that ends in the diseased streets of Calcutta." We must be realistic and recognize and deal with our bodily needs for food, sex, and exercise.

Biofeedback and any combination of the techniques that incorporate the mind and the body would seem to offer the greatest assistance. As you may have noticed, in addition to the relaxation response, some of the exercises we have offered here incorporate yoga stretches. In his work with patients, Dr. Sedlacek is using dance therapy, which is group-oriented and employs movements designed specifically for the particular person's physique. We firmly believe that the combination of mental and physical exercises will give us the best opportunity to deal effectively with stress and to enjoy life to the fullest.

Further research and practical experience will help us to delineate how and when to apply these general techniques for stress reduction as preventive measures, as well as helping to create new ways of using biofeedback, the relaxation response, TM, yoga, and dance therapy as treatments in themselves or in conjunction with other therapies (psychotherapy, medication, and surgery). What is clear is that through the use of machines to feed back information about our bodily responses, we will continue to learn about our body-mind relationship. As we learn more, we will be able to bring more stress-related diseases under control. One area that we think offers much promise is the work that is being done with children.

Perhaps stress-related disease goes hand in hand with a loss of spontaneity and joy. Drs. Wes Lynch and Neal Miller showed in their work that children could more easily show hand temperature increase than their parents. This work and another study done at Menninger may suggest that as we grow older, we are taught that we have no control over our internal body and its functioning—or cease to believe that we do.

It might be that this belief system is what prevents us from better controlling the health of our heart, arteries, pancreas (whose decreased output brings about the symptoms of diabetes), and brain (e.g., in epilepsy). Since we have been able to monitor these functions, we are learning a great deal about how symptoms evolve. Perhaps eventually we can develop methods of effecting a state of contentment by understanding the physical and emotional components of the mind-body relationship.

These developments are quite remarkable when we realize that it has been only in the last two or three years that we have had clear procedures for monitoring and treating the body with biofeedback. In biofeedback centers throughout the country, research and treatment are going on that will supply more and more evidence of what we as individuals can do for our own health.

In Atlanta, Dr. John V. Basmajian has done a great deal of work using the EMG. His book *Muscles Alive* is very informative. At Johns Hopkins University in Baltimore, Drs. Schuster and Engel continue their excellent work in heartrate control, hypertension, and fecal incontinence. In Philadelphia, Dr. Steve Padnes started one of the first biofeedback clinics. He is director of the Psychosomatic Service at Jefferson University. At Temple Medical School in Philadelphia excellent work is also being done on muscular rehabilitation.

Dr. Miller's group at Rockefeller University in New York City continues to do basic research. At New York University, Dr. Joseph Brudny treats spastic torticollis and other problems requiring muscular rehabilitation. At St. Luke's Hospital, Dr. Sedlacek's research and treatment of hypertension and clinical treatment for migraine, tension headache, and Raynaud's disease continues. Dr. Sedlacek also uses biofeedback for relaxation, treatment of sexual dysfunctions, anxiety, and other stress-related problems in short-term psychotherapy.

In Hartford, Drs. Stroebel and Gluck have established a clinic for treatment of migraine and tension headaches and Raynaud's disease. They are also doing research on the treatment of hypertension and colitis. Dr. Johann Stoyva continues his research work at the University of Colorado Medical Center as well as being editor of the new journal put out by the Biofeedback Research Society (*Biofeedback and Self-Regulation*). Dr. Tom Budzynski continues his research and treatment at the Biofeedback Institute of Denver.

In other centers in Massachusetts, Illinois, Texas, California and other states, both basic research and clinical treatments are under study. In California, the state biofeedback society is now offering certified training courses in an effort to standardize biofeedback treatment.

What of the future? It appears that there will be other modern clinics where stress-related diseases will be identified, studied, and treated. Together doctors from different specialties and training, such as psychosomatic medicine, rehabilitation medicine, internal medicine, and behavior therapy, will practice more preventive medicine. The physical examination will employ such recording devices as the thermister, GSR, EEG, and EMG, to detect the first stages of disease or pathology.

People with stress-related diseases will profit from these studies before beginning treatment, because their doctors will have more data from which to choose the best form of treatment. Doctors will also be able to give patients a better idea of how long the treatment (weeks, months, years) will take.

In the future, cases such as Joe's peptic ulcer will rarely happen if people become aware that they can self-regulate, that is, prevent, much of the damage that is caused by poorly handled stress. In potential cases of stroke and spastic torticollis, patients would seek treatment as soon as the first early warning physical symptoms have appeared, thus minimizing psychological and physical damage. Executives would be taught to deal more creatively with problems and to be aware of the negative strain on them and their colleagues.

Industry can help by providing "relaxation" rooms where employees can practice relaxation exercises instead of taking a coffee break. In China, the workers exercise before and during work. Here in the United States, people generally stop getting reinforcement for exercise when gym classes stop in high school or college. Most distressing, however, is the fact that often our children in the earliest school grades do not have any planned exercise. Each child should be taught some method of relaxation as well as being given the opportunity to engage in some physical exercise daily.

One of the greatest side benefits of teaching stress prevention is that it involves the patients in their own health. The more they see that they can affect their own health, the more they are capable of doing. Such productive patient involvement encourages patients to take further responsibility for their physical and mental well-being through regular relaxation and exercise, which will give them the physical serenity and energy needed to deal with their problems.

The medical profession, with the exception of analysts, has not paid sufficient attention to how the patient's "will" can affect his health. Yet there are numerous cases in which the patient's determination to live or to overcome disease appears to be the factor that effects a cure. Doctors have seen or heard of the parent who has been told that he or she has only six months to live but who is determined to see his or her children finish their schooling or get married—and does. The patient dies only after the awaited event has taken place.

To cite a more "scientific" example, Dr. Carl Simonton is using mental imagery to help cancer patients. Dr. Simonton is a radiologist who uses the usual x-ray therapy, but he also feels that "we all create sickness to solve emotional conflicts. The cancer victim is no more to blame for self-inducing his cancer than is the person who gets a cold to avoid a stressful situation at work."*

He has his patients imagine that their white cells (part of the body's defense or immune system) are very strong and aggressive. They then imagine these white cells attacking and destroying the cancer cells. He thus supports and encourages the patient to use his own immune (defense) system to destroy cancer cells, causing a remission or cure. His results with hundreds of patients are very encouraging. His method takes advantage of the system's own striving for the dominance of normal cells.

There is also work demonstrating that cancer patients have certain characteristics and personalities that differ from those of noncancer patients. Cancer patients often deny feelings of hostility and have been found to have endured greater hardships than most before the age of 7. A recent editorial in the *Journal of the American Medical Association* cited research that showed that chronic stress was related to a greater frequency of cancer in mice.†

---

*In K. Hanson, "Some Doctors Prescribe Faith, Plus Pills," *Daily News*, September 19, 1975, p. 41.
†"Animal Study Shows Intriguing Link Between Chronic Stress and Cancer," *Journal of the American Medical Association*, vol. 233, August 18, 1975, pp. 757-759.

Other researchers are working on a preventive measure (a vaccine) against cancer.

This data would suggest that some cases of cancer are related to chronic stress, and a decrease in coping behavior at the cellular level, that is, decreased resistance to cancer growth.

In essence, what any medical treatment also may have to include is the altering of the patient's belief about his or her disease or distress. In the case of cancer we can try to change patients' feelings of helplessness by showing them the possibility of consciously activating their immunization system. Influence at the cellular level is only one step removed from what we are doing now in learning to direct our blood flow to various parts of the body.

Certainly our experience and that of others with biofeedback and passive volition support this proposition. In fact, biofeedback may be the first medical method in modern times that places the patient in this position of consciously using his own psychophysiological system to "heal" disease.

Dr. Jerome Frank, professor emeritus of psychiatry of the Johns Hopkins University School of Medicine, has stated that "although psychological forces cannot replace the healing powers of Western medicine, they can enhance treatment effectiveness." He feels that "the psychological approach to treatment should be integrated with the diagnostic and therapeutic tools of modern medical science to yield a more unified system of healing."* Further application of biofeedback techniques and stress

---

*J. Frank, "Confirming Psychological Approach with Medicine Would Unify Therapy System," *Clinical Psychiatry News*, September 1975, p. 2.

management should provide greater advancement in this direction.

Perhaps recognition of the need for biological self-regulation will generalize to recognition of the need to take a more responsible role in such areas as politics, education, and ecology. The more we get in touch with our true selves, the more we can get in touch with the needs of others, from individual health to the health of society. Perhaps the change of consciousness we discussed earlier will come about through each of us becoming responsible for ourselves.

We ask you to join us in beginning to deal more effectively with stress by using the exercises and suggestions in this book to improve your mental and physical well-being. It is hoped that these efforts will help us to bring about the further changes that are desperately needed in our individual consciousness as well as in our society.

Appendix

REPORTED HEADACHE SUBSTANCES

Seasonings

A-1 Steak Sauce and variants
Meat tenderizer
Monosodium glutamate ("Accent")
Salt (use instead Morton's "Lite Salt")
Soy sauce
Worcestershire sauce and variants

Beverages

Beer
Champagne
Coffee (limit to 3 cups per day, check for chocolate content)
Cola drinks
Milk products
Red wines (Burgundy Chianti, etc.)

Foods

Aged beef
Anchovies
Bacon
Broad bean pods
Canned figs
Cheese (aged or strong types, esp. cheddar)
Chicken livers
Chinese foods
Chocolate
Citrus fruits
Corn
Eggs
Ham
Hot dogs
Liver
Nuts
Olives
Onions
Peanut butter
Peas
Pork
Pickled herring
Raisins
Salami
Sour cream
Wheat

Sources: D. J. Dalessio and F. Speer, *Journal of the American Medical Association,* vol. 232, no. 4, April 28, 1975, p. 400; and C. Stroebel, Institute for Living, Hartford, Conn., personal communication.

Suggested Reading

Benson, H. *The Relaxation Response.* New York, William Morrow, 1975.

Bernstein, C., and Woodward, B. *All the President's Men.* New York, Warner, 1974.

Birk, L. *Biofeedback: Behavioral Medicine.* New York, Grune & Stratton, 1973.

Blomfield, H., Cain, M., and Jaffe, D. *TM— Transcendental Meditation.* Delacorte Press, 1975.

DiCara, L., ed. *Limbic and Autonomic Nervous Systems Research.* New York, Plenum Press, 1974.

Duara, L., Barber, T., Miller, N., Shapiro, D., and Stoyva, J., eds. *Biofeedback and Self-Control.* An Aldine Annual on the Regulation of Bodily Processes and Consciousness. Chicago, Aldine, 1970–75.

Friedman, M., and Rosenman, R. *Type A Behavior and Your Heart.* Greenwich, Conn., Fawcett, 1974.

Greenfield, N., and Steinback, R. *Handbook of Psychophysiology.* New York, Holt, Rinehart and Winston, 1972.

Grinker, R. *Psychosomatic Concepts.* New York, Aronson, 1973.

Rubin, V., and Comitas, L. *Ganga in Jamaica.* Paris, Mouton, 1975.

Selye, H. *Stress Without Distress.* New York, Lippincott, 1974.

Vande Wiele, L., and Richart, R. *Biorhythms and Human Reproduction.* New York, Wiley, 1974.

Welch, B., and Welch, Λ. *Physiological Effects of Noise.* New York, Plenum Press, 1970.

Wolff, H. *Wolff's Headache and Other Pain.* 3rd ed., rev. by D. Dalessio. New York, Oxford Press, 1972.

Index